Keeping Time

Keeping Time

a life making music

To Nancy — who is seen and also makes beautiful music. A great partner! Love

Ann Copeland

[signature]

Shanti Arts Publishing

Brunswick, Maine

Keeping Time
A Life Making Music

Published by Shanti Arts Publishing
Interior and cover design by Shanti Arts Designs

Shanti Arts LLC
193 Hillside Road
Brunswick, Maine 04011

shantiarts.com

Cover image: alzay/istockphoto.com/459593411
Frontispiece: Josh Edelman, *Author's Hands at the Piano*, 2018
Interior image: Miroslava Hlavacova/shutterstock.com/ 141359635

Printed in the United States of America

ISBN: 978-1-947067-55-4 (softcover)
ISBN: 978-1-947067-56-1 (digital)

Library of Congress Control Number: 2018958670

for
Julian Snow. a rare teacher

and

Gretchen Moon, piano partner for nineteen years

It is not music's function to express rational necessities. The human spirit has commissioned the human voice to appear in two languages. One to serve man's intellect and purpose; the other to serve his sentiment and his transcendental urge.

— Artur Schnabel

CONTENTS

Acknowledgments

I thank those who read preliminary sections of some essays: Sue Duggan Kane, Helen Braden, Elizabeth Seibert, and Gail McCowen. At a later stage, all of these pages profited from Anne Bowden's tactful, incisive suggestions, and from Judi Chien's talent for precision. John Corenswet's professional editorial eye also helped me sharpen many pages of each essay.

Most of all, however, it has been the experience of making music with friends — Barbara Bonnem (violin), Elizabeth Seibert (violin and flute), Elizabeth Keyser (piano), George Struble (cello), Claire Furtwangler (piano and cello), Nancy Lodge (flute), John Poole (piano), Deborah Patterson (piano and voice), Maribeth Kallemeyn (piano), Judi Chien (voice), Patricia Alley (piano), Barbara Johnson (piano), four-hand partner Gretchen Moon, and my husband, Al (banjo) — that shored up faltering confidence and enabled me to persevere in seeking words to honor years of delight through musicking.

Grateful acknowledgment is made to the editors of the following publications in which these essays first appeared:

"Strange Relation," *Image*, No. 42, Spring/Summer 2004; "An Evening at the Piano," *Open Spaces*, Summer 2006; "Six Bagatelles for Dancers," *The Iowa Review*, Fall 2006; "Reunion," *Tiferet*, Winter 2006; "Improvising," *Fourth Genre*, Fall 2007; "Of Dissonance and Touch: A Movement in Sonata Form," *Image*, No.52, Winter 2007; "Pré-d'en-Haut," *The Fiddlehead*, No. 269, Autumn 2016; "Composing for Claire," *Still Point Arts Quarterly*, No. 26, Summer 2017.

Introduction

Long years of making music have offered me release, challenge, solace, collaboration, glimpses of possibility, a perishable entrance into felt mystery, and the chance to create a gift with and for others.

As I write these words, planet Earth has been my home for over eighty-four years. That mountain of yesterdays has seen me as a teacher, a vowed religious, a wife, a mother, a fiction writer, and has witnessed decades of my dedicated amateur music-making, alone or with others, in chapels, living rooms, and schools; in settings foreign or domestic, intimate or exposed; in mental states anxious, playful, or grieving.

Time's gift remains alive in me as I write this, just home from joining friends for two hours to sight-read a Pleyel composition for two violins and piano, after earlier relishing Mozart four-hand sonatas with my piano partner of years. I take such moments as privileged gifts.

In 2004, recently retired after decades of teaching and writing, a powerful, unexpected urge seized me: Leave aside the languishing long novel-in-process and devote yourself to writing about the cumulative effect of making music over a long and varied life.

BUT ... as a reader and a writer, I had never favored memoir, preferring instead to observe life's dazzle and create fictions about it.

ALSO . . . music is notoriously difficult to write about. However, I wanted to write not about music in the abstract, but about making music in its many forms: composing, playing, arranging, partnering, studying, improvising.

A tale of many parts.

The urge persisted.

Then there was the "long and varied life" part. The tale did not lend itself to narrative forms of fiction.

Perhaps if I centered these moments within my own days, explored them in settings as disparate as a chilly chapel where, as a monastic nun, I loved to chant Gregorian and my decades-later attempts to compose Gregorian blues, perhaps then it could add up to a whole story. Or I could link my fourteen years of composing annual birthday songs for a granddaughter with my childhood experiences of learning to play piano. Well, this would become a tale twisting and turning and sometimes tangled, but animated, always, by a deep musical connection.

Prompted by the surprise of seeing a framed reproduction of Gregorian chant in the home of pious Jewish friends in Washington, I began the first essay. Afterward, I named it "Strange Relation." Life's nonsense pierces us with strange relation. Wallace Stevens had it right.

The urge grew stronger, along with its challenges. How could the thrill of seeing a limited fourteen-year-old son execute with rare style his dancing powers in a small Nova Scotia hall link to my thrill as a twelve year old dancing at the Starlight Roof in Manhattan in 1945 with my father who would die soon thereafter? How to link this woman in a religious habit thrilling to flamenco dancing at the Spanish Pavilion of the 1965 World's Fair to high school afternoons many years earlier when, in a Connecticut living room, my widowed mother and I would kick off shoes, drop the needle, and execute a breathless Charleston?

Pages mounted up. Time passed. Throughout these many years of writing, Proust's words have again and again rung true: "The nimble shuttles of the years weave links between those of our memories which seem at first most independent of each other."[1]

With growing curiosity I searched out the harmonic changes that underscored my particular dance of life. As I wrote I came to realize that, despite its variety and discontinuities, my sense of time here did not feel frayed or fragmented. Despite dissonances aplenty, it felt organic, a strong continuity threading through its parts. I sought to illumine that thread. Surely that sense of organic continuity has been created partly by years of musicking.

Since this could not be a straightforward "then and then and then" life narrative, the brief life summary below may help you weave your own understanding of the when and where of each essay. Sprinkled in between longer essays I've placed shorter pieces, "ornaments" I call them, to round out my story of how making music can release and bind and create radiant delays in the days of our inevitable passing.

In the final analysis I rediscovered quite simply the sheer joy of creating, of having fun, of savoring imperfection, of surviving risk, of accepting challenge, of laughing at impossibility, of learning with and from others.

Long years of making music have offered me release, challenge, solace, collaboration, glimpses of possibility, a perishable entrance into felt mystery, and the chance to create a gift with and for others.

I hope to share some of that gift with you through my story of *Keeping Time*.

LIFE STORY, WITH MENTION OF RELEVANT ESSAYS

Early Years and Education

1932   I was born Virginia Walsh into a devoted Irish Roman Catholic family in Hartford, Connecticut.

1938–50   I attended Catholic grammar and high schools in Waterbury, Connecticut. I began piano lessons in second grade. My father died when I was thirteen. (cf. "Six Bagatelles," "Composing for Claire," "Learning to Play," "Of Dissonance and Touch")

1954   I graduated from the College of New Rochelle. (cf. "Reunion," "Composition Blues") Two months later I answered a call felt for many years and entered the Ursuline Order.

Training and Teaching as an Ursuline

1954–57   I completed the novitiate and made first profession (temporary vows) as an Ursuline in Beacon, New York. (cf. "Strange Relation," "Reunion," "Variations")

1957–59   I went through further formation at the Ursuline House of Studies in Washington, D.C. I completed an M.A. in English at Catholic University.

1959   I made final vows as an Ursuline in Washington, D.C.

Teaching Years

1959–61   At the Ursuline School, Bethesda, Maryland, I

taught English and Latin, trained the Choral Club, and played organ. (cf. "Composition Blues," "Of Dissonance and Touch")

1961–63   I taught English, economic geography, and liturgical music at Mount St. Ursula, Bronx, New York. (cf. "Of Dissonance and Touch," "Composition Blues")

1963–66   I was an instructor of English at the College of New Rochelle. (cf. "Reunion")

1966   I became a Ph.D. candidate in English at Cornell University.

1967   While at Cornell, I sought release from vows and re-entered secular life.

1967   I took my first trip as a secular adult, to Michelstadt, Germany. (cf. "Ornaments," "A Grace Note")

1968   I married Albert Furtwangler and moved to Chicago. ("Strange Relation")

1968–70   I received the Ph.D. in English from Cornell University; Wallace Stevens was the subject of my dissertation.

Wife, Mother, Teacher, Writer

1969–70   I was an instructor of English at Indiana University Northwest, Gary, Indiana.

1970   My son Tom was born. (cf. "Strange Relation")

1971   With my husband and son, I moved to New

Brunswick, Canada. I held various adjunct university teaching jobs during my years in Canada. (cf. "Six Bagatelles," "Salute to Morning," "A Golden Escape," "Pré-d'en-Haut," "Partnering")

1974   We adopted my son Andrew. (cf. "Six Bagatelles," "Of Dissonance and Touch")

1974–96   During these years, I became a fiction writer, completing several books that were published. I also held stints as a visiting fiction writer in Caldwell, Idaho; Moscow, Idaho; Wichita, Kansas; McMinnville, Oregon; Halifax, Nova Scotia; and Fredericton, New Brunswick.

1996–99   I taught at Willamette University in Salem, Oregon, as Professor of English Literature and Writing, holding the inaugural Hallie Ford Chair in Writing.

Retirement from Teaching

During my retirement years, I wanted to learn more about music and to make more music. I longed to be freed from notation. I began to study improvisation with a gifted teacher. A talented four-hand pianist found me, and we became weekly partners. I took a course on Beethoven, practiced and played on my newly acquired Steinway, made music with my husband on banjo, and increased the already familiar pleasure of making music with others. The works of Christopher Small — *Music and the Common Tongue* and *Musicking* — deeply interested me. Inspired by his work, I decided to try writing about my own experience of musicking.

As I played, I kept on writing these essays.

STRANGE RELATION

My trail of anecdotes stretches far apart in time and setting: from chilly chapels, to an apartment floor in Hyde Park, to a salesman's table at Marshall Field's, to a hospitable home in Washington, to a music department rehearsal room in Salem, Oregon. The trail honors forms of attraction and appetite for color, for music, for composing of several kinds. Strange relations indeed.

That I begin my book of musical memories not with music but with color suggests how unpredictable and interwoven have been the threads of music-making in my life. This first thread unexpectedly brought me, by way of color, back to music.

It was sixteen months since I had left religious life and re-entered the world of color, though re-inhabited might be a better word. Color, of course, had surrounded me even in my convent years: the earth, sky, clouds, and all of nature's bounty were not bound by persistent black-and-whiteness. Re-inhabit, though, means that not only was I, as my new husband would say, appearing once again in technicolor, but that my new domestic setting was inviting color. As we wondered what dishes or sheets or blankets to buy for out first apartment in Chicago's Hyde Park, I could now imagine in color. When I went — as I did for the first time in fourteen years — to the grocery store, I could walk rainbow aisles of cans, cereal boxes, pop bottles, and toilet paper, and choose my shade. Suddenly, my daily universe demanded coloring.

All of this dazzled, and there rose in me a raging appetite for color, generating excitement, release, a thrilling sense of adventure. In a burst of ambition and supposed frugality, I asked my mother to send my old sewing machine from home. Determined, I set about learning again how to use it. My last significant effort had been fourteen years before with an old treadle machine in the novitiate.

Fresh from college graduation in June 1954, ten of us had chosen to respond to the call to religious life. On a hot July day, we entered the Ursuline novitiate in Beacon, New York, eager to embark on our training as postulants. For the first six months, as we learned this new way of life, we would strive to demonstrate our suitability for admission to the Ursuline Order. If we made that hurdle, we would receive part of the religious habit in a formal clothing ceremony the following January and become novices for two years while we studied and practiced the vows, prayers, and rules of spiritual life. At the end of these years, if accepted to profession in the Ursuline Order, we would make temporary vows, receive the black veil and crucifix, and be sent either for further schooling or to teach in some school in the Northeast. Three years later, if we persevered, would come final profession, perpetual vows, and the ring.

For now, among our many assigned tasks, one issued a particular challenge: In October, we postulants were told that during the four weeks of Advent we would each make our own floor-length habit for the January clothing ceremony. Yards and yards of black serge faced us to be transformed into the religious garment we so yearned to wear — yoke, pleats, voluminous sleeves, and all. Wondrously, our superior's command seemed to bestow ability. With minimal instruction and a great deal of ripping, each of us did as ordered, though the yoke was not sweet nor the burden light. We laid out swathes of the black material on the long novitiate-room tables. We measured, snipped, pinned, basted, hoped, and prayed. In silence — with a sneaked whisper here and there — we somehow managed to complete our habits in time to don them at the January clothing ceremony after we shed the wedding dresses borrowed for the occasion.

And now I found myself in yet another life, heeding the insistent call of color, equipped with my own sewing machine, an apartment with lots of empty floor space for laying out bits and pieces, and hours alone while my husband was off teaching at the university. I could distract myself from the dissertation I should have been working on by facing a different test. Titillated by Marimekko designs and teased by pattern books, I spent hours flipping pages, imagining my new self in this, in that, inventing my own extended clothing ceremony in technicolor. I could go round the corner from South Hyde Park Boulevard, climb on the 54th Street El, whiz down to Marshall Field's, and happily graze in pastures of color, texture, design: the fabulous fabric department. On the desk in the study back home, Wallace Stevens's poetic ballet with the meaning of meaning paled to insignificance before these tactile enticements. Dull print, black and white; he could wait.

Roll on roll of fabric invited my touch. I loved to walk between rows of display, gaze at them, finger the weave, the nub, the soft or taut surfaces, feel enclosed by all that color that might be made into just about anything . . . in theory. People speak of salivating at the sight of chocolate, and I know something of that, too, but in those days, I salivated at the sight of colored cloth radiant with possibility. I poked through remnant piles for bright pieces to fringe into covers and napkins for the table we had created from an unfinished door purchased at a lumber yard.

Appetite and imagination far outstripped my capacity to do the work. Before the novitiate habit-making challenge, my one venture into sewing had been in eighth grade: a brief course at the local YWCA that resulted in an apron of unbleached cotton with red trim that I proudly presented to my mother for Christmas. I don't remember her ever using it. Now I aimed to create clothing I would actually wear. I worked away — snipping, pinning, basting — all the time suppressing guilt about avoiding Stevens. The luxurious gold and black cape with a black satin lining that I eventually produced to cover my expanding womb made me feel positively regal. Another dress, made from what I hadn't realized was upholstery material, saw me effectively through nine months' expansion. It hung about me stiff and heavy, its muted shades of burgundy, green, gray, and black blending into a multicolored tent. My long-ago lesson in gathering pleats and attaching them to a yoke turned out to be useful for draping this non-virgin about to become a mother. My favorite number featured red, blue, black, yellow, and green stripes, and it transformed me into a walking box of Crayola crayons.

When a slimmer me finally returned to face black print on white pages, another dress, of blue and white piqué, saw me through my orals. For some months, however, I ducked the call of Wallace Stevens's verbal games, always waiting in the study just the other side of the living room, so hopefully strewn with my own compositions.

From those early married months in Chicago, those days of excited forays into fabric, one moment stands forth with a peculiar power, a thread still vibrant over five decades later.

The year is 1970. I am in Marshall Field's on State Street, Chicago. Driven by this persistent appetite for color and cloth, I have just wandered those fields on the fabric floor. Replenished, I dream my way back to the escalator and head down.

Ahead of me, close to the bottom of the escalator, a man is busily selling items to a small crowd. He holds up before them what appear to be pieces of parchment with red staff lines on them, some with elaborately colored decorations and small black squares going up and down on the red lines. I know that four-line staff. I know those square-shaped notes called neumes. I know the curves of melody, arsis, and thesis. I have more than a nodding acquaintance with the eight church modes.

"These, framed, would make a beautiful object of interest in your dining room," he says. "A real conversation piece."

Cloth, color, texture, design: all evaporate. Years dissolve.

In the novitiate, I labored to learn that staff; to recognize the do clef, the fa clef; to decipher the rhythmic implications of the ictus; to accommodate voice and breath to the sense of Latin words; to relinquish self and merge my voice with others as instructed by my *Liber Usualis*: "In order that all the voices may be one, which is most essential, each singer should attempt in all modesty to allow his own voice to become merged in the volume of sound of the choir as a whole." After I finally donned my own freshly made novice's habit, I was assigned to train younger sisters in the chant. Still later, as a community member in three successive houses, I was assigned to help convent choirs elicit from those strange black shapes the beauties of the Divine Office and liturgies for the celebration of Mass: sung prayer lifted in one voice toward a heaven that surely heard. Always feeling myself untrained at this, I puzzled over quilismas and episemas, pondered the mysteries of the podatus, tonus peregrinus, and cadence . . . because I was told to.

There came years even later when, having learned how to translate that ancient code into numbers so our students could sing the chant, I would stand in front of our high school assembly for weekly Mass and earnestly wave my draped black sleeves, curving arsis and thesis in midair, encouraging their young voices — more attuned to the Beatles, whom I had never heard — to strive for that pure unison. And how many decades before that had a much earlier self sat as a parochial school child at Sunday Mass in my own parish church in Waterbury, Connecticut, joining with children around me to sing the Eighth Ordinary and Third Credo while Sister eagle-eyed us from the end of the pew.

No doubt about it, that strange clef, those odd shapes, and the otherworldly beauty they signified cut deep into my soul over many years.

Now, on the table before the salesman in Marshall Field's lies a pile of parchments, a cache of hidden treasure he obviously cannot assess.

I am instantly drawn. I ask if I may poke through the pile. Certainly.

Oh, here they are in bits and pieces, so many antiphons, hymns, sequences, and parts of psalms I've chanted over the years through weather hot or cold, in chapels drafty or stifling, eyes down, mind focused in the beginning years to make sense of the Latin. Then, after the Second Vatican Council required vernacular translation, I reveled in the more easily understood words of the psalmist. Sometimes with aching backs, addled brains, weary psyches, always clad in ankle-length black, we gathered in chapel to chant the Divine Office. It sanctified our days, our work. It effected an eternal measurement of time. At the first sound of the bell, we left work in the novitiate garden; we left high school and college classrooms; we left books open on our desks, papers half-corrected, apples half-peeled; we filed into chapel in silence and joined our voices, young and old, to the ancient, seemingly eternal voice of the psalmist crying to heaven.

So here it is with no warning smack in the middle of Marshall Field's: my very own madeleine. No taste, no smell, no little Proustian cupcake, just notes of Gregorian on a familiar staff with that odd little clasp on the left, and I am back in that black-and-white world. As customers brush past me, mildly curious, intent on their own goals, the wonder world of fabric is only one floor above, but I have forgotten it.

Quietly, almost inaudibly, I start to sing. It is an instinctive response.

Those neumes so carefully etched on the old parchment by some industrious monk or scribe were meant to be chanted in an atmosphere of worshipful prayer. These brittle pages before me were part of the breviary, the ancient revered book of hymns, prayers, and psalms read or chanted in monasteries ancient and modern, and daily recited by priests to this day. Someone had torn them out, dismembered the book. I can't sing it here in the middle of a shopping day on State Street in Chicago, Illinois. That isn't even in my mind. But the notes are there, calling. That's all there is to it. I try a few bars, the start of a hymn, as I rummage through the pieces of disassembled book for a text and melody that draw me. Others elbow, but I persist. I must have one.

Ah, here is one I have always loved. It is intact, the whole sequence, part of it on the front of the vellum, part on the back. The *Veni Sancte Spiritus*. Less colorful than some of the other fragments with their elaborately illuminated initial letters, it is, nonetheless, complete. The initial letter of each verse is done in alternating red and blue. What better plea from the midst of consumer heaven could this color-crazy consumer make than "Come Holy Spirit"? Pentecost has long been my favorite feast. I love the notion of a power mysteriously taking over and transforming one, be it by fire, or breath, or a holy spirit. He did it in color too. With pizazz. Flames of fire above their heads. And so I sing the whole thing.

Veni Sancte Spiritus	Come, Holy Spirit,
et emitte caelitus	send forth the heavenly
lucis tuae radium.	radiance of your light.

I sing quietly, amid abundance.

Veni, pater pauperum,	Come father of the poor,
veni, dator munerum,	come giver of gifts,
veni, lumen cordium.	come light of hearts.

Consolator optime,	Greatest consoler,
dulcis hospes animae,	sweet guest of the soul,
dulce refrigerium.	pilgrim's sweet relief.

Just days ago, I listened over the radio to accounts of the Kent State killings. And now, at the university here, students threaten to take over the administration building.

Consolator optime,	Greatest consoler,

Every week, desperate young men secretly head for Canada.

A few people nearby seem to be listening to me. I'm not a particularly good singer, but I do know how to make these lines work. Years of weekly choir rehearsal and daily chanting of the Hours have liberated some capacities.

In labore requies,	In labor, rest,
in aestu temperies,	in heat, temperance,
in fletu solatium.	in tears, solace.

How long, I wonder now, will my own labor be? These days, I am afraid to go alone at dusk through the streets of Hyde Park. South of there, Black Panthers roam.

I go on singing.

I am afraid to go alone to the shore of Lake Michigan after a frightening encounter there with a man. He came too close. I motioned to an imaginary husband resting under a nearby tree. My intimidator left.

I go on singing.

Flecte quod est rigidum,	Bend that which is rigid,
fove quod est frigidum,	fire that which is chilled,
rege quod est devium.	correct what goes astray.

Out of curiosity, I attended a City Council meeting run by Mayor Daley. When he didn't want to listen to the Hyde Park alderman, he turned off the mike, reduced his adversary to silent babble, and sat imperturbably up there on his dais like a little pope.

My voice sounds feeble and shaky.

No tongues of fire descend.

I turn to the back of the vellum. This side is not as beautiful.

Da virtutis meritum,	Grant us Thy grace in life,
da salutis exitum,	that we may die and ever be
da perenne gaudium.	in eternal joy.

Amen. Alleluia. Amen.

Perenne or not, I'm all for *gaudium.*

I am there in color. I am there in black and white.

The transept is around me, the spartan choir stalls, the black-and-white figures next to me and across from me, my voice joining theirs. This powerful stirring to life, this unsought surging upward from the past, the echo from a deeper self, the longing to give it voice — what is this?

Perhaps the secular surroundings prompted some of that urgency. I could have stood there mute, mentally singing, the way one browses through print here and there in a bookstore. But no. The chant so beautifully inscribed on that vellum, the words beneath it called for voice, for sung prayer.

I bought the parchment for fifteen dollars. Later, in the Strand Bookstore in New York City, I would see less beautiful, incomplete pieces for $250.

We framed it with both sides of the sequence visible to be read or sung. It now hangs next to my grand piano, which these days issues a far stronger call than color, or cloth, or even print.

While I struggle to articulate a line of keyboard music or try to figure out just how one chord relates to the next, above me hangs a cry to the Holy Spirit: *Veni Sancte Spiritus*.

That seems just right. I need all the help I can get.

"Life's nonsense pierces us with strange relation."[2]

I have Stevens to thank for that line. The strangeness of what links parts of our lives, how we feel and understand the meaning of these links, informs my trail of anecdotes here. And so, by way of strange relation comes another turn to the story of chant and color. It occurs thirty-one years after the impromptu moment at Marshall Field's.

Some years ago, my husband and I visited a cherished fourth-grade teacher of his, now sadly moving away from recognition and memory into the world of Alzheimer's. His wife had set a beautiful lunch for us in their bright apartment on Whidby Island, Washington. Surrounded by signs of a long, richly cultivated life together and deep mutual devotedness, we shared a memorable meal and tried to suppress sadness.

Afterward, as we prepared to leave, I was stopped by a large framed piece on the wall straight ahead of me. Gregorian chant. I read it quickly, mentally hearing what was clearly the beginning of an Introit. This time I didn't sing out loud. It might be the beginning of the Introit for the Third Mass of Christmas, I thought. I wasn't sure. Midway down the left side of the page — paper painted to simulate vellum, not the crinkly vellum of my *Veni Sancte Spiritus* — a large inset square of gold held a brilliantly decorated H, the first letter of *Hodie nata est*. I hummed tentatively. The text was incomplete in a way these pieces can be, but I seemed to recognize the curve of the melody on the five red staff lines. The five lines instead of four suggested a later work of art, not torn from a breviary but created to appear that way. And if the text really was from the Third Mass of Christmas, the *nata* should be *natus*, but perhaps the monk nodded off or the artist didn't know his Latin. In any case, the piece was quite beautiful.

What on earth was this doing here in the home of pious Jews? He had been for many years a cantor in their congregation. Was he perhaps aware that historians understand Gregorian chant to have originated from ancient Jewish synagogue tradition? Did he know what my *Harvard Dictionary of Music* tells me? Jewish peoples living in isolated areas today — Saudi Arabia, Iran — still sing melodies strikingly similar to Gregorian chant.

My hostess saw my delight and surprise.

"How come?" I asked her. "And I think it might be from the Introit of one of the Christmas Masses, of all things!"

She laughed with pleasure. Others had wondered about their having it in their home. She said that she and her husband had been attracted to it years ago. It was that simple. They found the whole colorful composition extraordinarily beautiful. "But you know its meaning," she said. She knew my story and had read my book about convent life.

We gathered our things to leave, a sad final parting.

She took me aside. "I want you to have this," she said, pointing to the Gregorian composition in its large gold frame. "You understand it. We have enjoyed it. We cannot keep it forever. It would mean a great deal to us both to know that you have it."

The world we inhabit abounds with empty gestures. In the instant of her offer, though, her impulse felt so solidly grounded. It honored a tie that transcended lesser barriers, those of belief, ideology, background, and spiritual lineage. It was a recognition of friendship wrapped in a colorful code of Gregorian chant. I never hesitated for an instant, though I could see my husband wondering. We had come to give, not take. We had come out of deep gratitude and affection toward a man whose gift through teaching had spanned decades and profoundly touched an earlier life.

No matter. Beyond the giving and the taking shimmered a gesture that transformed the moment. "This chant has special meaning for you. I want you to have it."

We took it home.

In only a few instances in my life can I recall an offering so spontaneous, so aware, so right.

Then began the search to identify it. After we got home, I took down my *Liber Usualis* from the shelf in my study. *Hodie nata est.* Today is born. I flipped to the three Masses of Christmas. This was not from the Third Mass. The melody was wrong. I had somehow wanted it to be from Christmas. Could it be a hymn? I checked these. No. An antiphon? No. Finally, I began to go through the two thousand tissue-thin pages of a thick, black book that saw me through thirteen years, from chapel to chapel, from house to house, from early dedication and certitude to growing perplexity and doubt. So many vestiges of that former life have vanished, yet this book remains, its pages covered with neumes and Latin, the priceless compendium of hymns and psalms and sequences and lessons and masses, texts rich with meaning and history.

I hunted and hunted but have yet to find the source for those particular lines of chant.

We hung it in the dining room.

Halfway down the left side of the page, the beautiful H of *Hodie*, set in its square field of gold, houses an intricate design in red and green and gold and blue, the whole letter creating the effect of a flowering tree blooming upward, then bending over, green and blue leaves and red flowers caught forever in a graceful bow. The whole composition breathes color and life, as if the artist wanted to signal fecundity in a single letter, bless text with life, and show forth its rich blossoming. *Hodie.* Today.

Above my Steinway hangs a plea for the Holy Spirit to come and deliver his mysterious, much needed gifts.

Near our dining room table hangs a celebration of birth — *Hodie nata est* — an affirmation of new life today.

Breaking bread with those we love, attending to words in texts, lifting voices in sung prayer, making music together — such efforts link us invisibly as we each thread our way through time. Now and then, along each of our separate strands, a moment may light up with rare incandescence. Such moments offer solace strangely peace-giving.

Dulce refrigerium. The pilgrim's sweet relief.

As I write of peace-giving solace that can spring from moments of felt connection, the radio, the television, the omnipresent media pound us with reminders of danger and death: bombs, wars, drones, impending nuclear disaster. It feels a bit wistful to affirm the slender strength of Gregorian chant in the face of such evident power. Yet one way or another, through composings that color our lives, we forge links across time and weave connections to light our paths. Such links hold their own peculiar power. They can generate, as well, a hidden source of strength against the onslaughts of time.

Decades have passed since my formal departure from the world of Gregorian chant. Even now, so many years later, occasional visits to a Trappist or Benedictine monastery renew my sense that the chant holds something eternal, perhaps singing a human need too deep to express in any other way.

Fragile as my thread may seem — a curving line of neumes given voice by monk or choir in rarefied settings — a brief coda here supports my claim that this sung prayer gives voice to a reality urgent and deep, even in the era of super bombs.

Recently, I received a notice that a professor of music at a nearby university was to give a colloquium for students and faculty. Its title caught my attention: "Chants: Metamorphosis of a Composition." I knew him to be an outstanding teacher, composer, and jazz musician, as well as head of the music department. In 1995 he was commissioned to compose a piece for performance by the local chamber orchestra. That year he conducted the premiere of his composition, which was based on melodies from four different eleventh-century Gregorian chants. More recently, a summer grant enabled him to undertake transcribing for wind band the original orchestral composition. His presentation for this colloquium would focus on the chants themselves, the original compositional process and resulting work, and finally the transcription of the large work from the medium of chamber orchestra to contemporary wind band.

On a drizzly late January morning, he met an assembly of college students, music majors, and colleagues from his department and the university, plus a few interested outsiders like me.

By way of introduction, he explained something of his own musical background. As he put it, he grew up thinking it was normal that every Sunday he and his dad would sing in the church choir his mother directed, and every weekend, as well, he would listen to his father's jazz group rehearse at their home. His father was a band director and jazz trumpet player. Church singing, jazz improvisation, family talent, and shared music, years of education, and a persistent attraction to composing: from that matrix grew a professional life given to music in several forms.

Facing our assembly of assorted sleepy and hungry twenty-year-olds, he sought to account for his lifelong attraction to Gregorian chant. He summed it up in words something like this: "Maybe the attraction to the chants is that they are a means to bring us close to our own true selves, close to God. They are simple, pure, and they seem to me, more than any other kind of music, to express spiritual truth."

Honoring that attraction, he had turned to Gregorian chant as the source for his composing, hoping to discover interesting musical ideas that he could express in a new form.

From a cassette, he had selected three chants to work with: *Procedenten Sponsum, Veni Redemptor Gentium,* and *Dies Est Laetitiae.*

At this point, he played for us a tape of the original chants. Into the room on that drizzly morning floated the pure sound of voices raised in prayer sung along clear lines. No nave, no altar, no liturgical context, just that rare purity of voice and line echoing in the air. Students in jeans and backwards baseball caps, their backpacks crowding the aisles, their laps holding lunches soon to be consumed, a few listeners taking notes, others with eyes closed the better to hear; a far cry this from chilly chapel, erect black-and-white forms, or tired shoppers stopping to see what that odd pile of vellum might be on a table in Marshall Field's. Yet there it was, growing in the room as we listened: a pure sound rising, then falling, curving high, then dropping off; a voice that seemed to speak of something beyond lunch, beyond shopping, beyond political turmoil, beyond brutality, beyond time itself, yet very much grounded in time by the human voice.

For the rest of the hour, we listened to his compositions while he projected the scores on a screen. Occasionally, he interspersed a comment, but most of our effort consisted of looking at notation and listening. No doubt many of the music majors could decode some of the motifs, formulas, and structural devices that underlay his original orchestral composition. I was looking and listening hard, but more ignorantly. My own efforts to compose have been largely word centered, with only the occasional foray into composing pieces of music strictly for fun. Writers' work ends up as black print on white pages. When notated, the composers' work, as well, ends up as marks on a page. Both have their afterlife, though, and assume unexpected shapes in memory and imagination, becoming new creations. This morning was a living illustration of that fact.

He explained to us, "The challenges of the compositional

process were to create meaningful instrumental music for orchestra from vocal music that originated in and is used for an entirely different intent." This composing has nothing to do with text or liturgy.

In each composition, we could hear instruments echo, develop, and play with that original section of the chant. He gave a descriptor for each section derived from the chants: *Procedentem Sponsum* became "Fanfare and 6/8 Melody"; *Veni Redemptor Gentium* became "Mixed Meter Chant with Amen"; *Dies Est Laetitiae* became "Unison, Three Part Texture." These descriptors, as he called them, were not titles of movements or sections but simply descriptions of how he used each of the chants in the instrumental composition. The "Fanfare" featured, among other instruments, muted trombones and unmuted trumpet. Elsewhere in the composition, I was struck by other combinations: oboe with bassoon; a quasi-improvisational jazz development, a kind of "Gregorian Blues," as he remarked, a truly wonderful Amen; and finally, a grand restatement of the theme with the entire orchestra.

Listening to the orchestral effect with the chants still echoing in our memories was like seeing a lively, teasing spirit suddenly appear, then fade, only to reappear in a new color or dress, embedded suddenly in an unexpected texture of sound: appearances and vanishings daring, playful, subtle, engaging. Oddly, the phenomenon reminded me of the closing lines of Wallace Stevens's "Angel Surrounded by Paysans," in which the poet gives voice to an "angel of reality" devoid of heavenly accoutrements such as "ashen wing," "wear of ore," "tepid aureole." The angelic voice goes on to tell us:

> I am one of you and being one of you
> Is being and knowing what I am and know.
>
> Yet I am the necessary angel of earth,
> Since, in my sight, you see the earth again,

Cleared of its stiff and stubborn, man-locked set,
And, in my hearing, you hear its tragic drone

Rise liquidly in liquid lingerings
Like watery words awash; like meanings said

By repetitions of half meanings. Am I not,
Myself, only half of a figure of a sort,

A figure half seen, or seen for a moment, a man
Of the mind, an apparition apparelled in

Apparels of such lightest look that a turn
Of my shoulder and quickly, too quickly, I am gone?

A fanciful connection, perhaps, but somehow apt. No need for liturgical texts here, no remnant of Latin syllables or psalmody. Orchestral colors sufficed to transmute ancient materials into something new, yet still with figures half-heard or heard for a moment in "liquid lingerings" of sound.

As we listened, we were looking at the score. Notation itself, black marks on a page, remained part of the whole experience. We were not monks chanting words integral to our way of life; we were students seeking to hear and understand a complex process of musical metamorphosis.

Even so, as we listened, we were participating in the strange afterlife of music itself, materially offered here through notation but transformed by our ears and minds, imaginations and memory into "liquid lingerings" of ancient prayer. How this transition from marks on a page to sounds in the air to journeys in memory takes place touches on the central experience of this initial essay.

The relation of text to musical composition has long been a tortured topic. Its complex history lies beyond my scope here. I do know, though, that if today I hum the *Veni Sancte Spiritus* with no words, the melodies still carry meaning for me. To what extent does that meaning derive from the melody itself or from being embedded in the liturgy of Pentecost, to say nothing of the specific appeal those pleas to the Holy Spirit still carry for me? In other words, I cannot assess just how inextricably text and music, liturgical context, plus the elaborations of memory, imagination, and belief are bound up in my personal responses to the chant. On the purely secular level, the same applies. How often, during our twenty-five years of living in Canada, did I stand at an opening ceremony while the orchestra launched into "God Save the Queen" and instantly substitute, mentally, the words of "My Country 'Tis of Thee." And even now, all these years later, were I to hear, unadorned by text, the melody of the Salve Regina, Te Deum, Credo, and many other bits of Gregorian that I chanted for years, I would instantly attach to the melody the words they called for, if I knew them.

How subtly interwoven in time are our strands of loss, of gain, of bright or dark memory, of meaning only later recognized.

My trail of anecdotes stretches far apart in time and setting: from chilly chapels, to an apartment floor in Hyde Park, to a salesman's table at Marshall Field's, to a hospitable home in Washington, to a music department rehearsal room in Salem, Oregon. The trail honors forms of attraction and appetite for color, for music, for composing of several kinds.

Strange relations indeed. Yet as these came together in my mind and I sought words to gather them into this piece, I felt again the significance of attraction and the fun of discovery. Attraction moves us. It vibrates at the heart of all composing: the desire to bring together elements old or worn or just now remembered and make of them something new. We saw this demonstrated in the rehearsal room that drizzly January morning as we moved beyond one "man-locked set" to a new composition.

In his little book, *Poetics of Music,* based on his 1947 Charles

Eliot Norton lectures at Harvard, Igor Stravinsky addresses this fundamental human drive. "All creation," he says, "presupposes at its origin a sort of appetite that is brought on by the foretaste of discovery. The foretaste of the creative act accompanies the intuitive grasp of an unknown entity already possessed but not yet intelligible."[3]

According to Stravinsky, then, I had already grasped that "unknown entity." The challenge was to somehow uncover it. And so, bit by bit, the trail followed leads to an unexpected discovery: what we thought was lost we may, if we're lucky, yet find again, in a new form.

One of the best music teachers I had, a teacher of jazz improvisation, concluded his course at Westminster Choir School in 1986 by reminding us: "All music is gestural."

Perhaps he meant that within a musical piece itself, composers, musicians, and teachers speak of the arc, the overall gesture of a given section or phrase. In context, however, Laurie Altman, himself teacher, composer, and musician, seemed to mean something more. Or perhaps he was simply meeting my own predisposition to understanding.

Colors fade, sounds disappear, words betray, cloth feeds the moth; in the end, appetite and gesture remain. New compositions will come into being: colorful clothes, paintings, songs, symphonies, books, black marks on writers' pages. They speak of the fundamental human desire to make. They speak of the power of human attraction. They create, as well, across time, links to other unknown lives. I like to think of the arc linking the monk laboring to inscribe his neumes on vellum to a voice that could release what lay hidden there; the composer exploring, nine centuries later, what waited in those chants; the wife recognizing a hidden linkage, then offering a bit from her life to be shared in a new way, quite literally, in a new composing of life around a table she will never see, in a home she will never visit.

A composer is an artificer of links. In lucky moments, we

discover that linkage. My finding the salesman at the bottom of the escalator was luck. My happening to read of the composer's lecture about the metamorphosis of chant was luck.

Pressures abound today to reinforce our sense of darkness and disconnectedness on many levels. Dead ends. Final losses. As I write these words, newspapers and TV carry tales of the looting and pillaging of the National Museum of Iraq whose records and artifacts recorded the history of a civilization that began to flourish on the fertile plains of Mesopotamia more than seven thousand years ago. Links have been broken, destroyed forever. Closer to the heart, in personal lives, there is no denying links broken, as any adult knows. A sense of disconnectedness is our human métier. A page is torn from a sacred book, a particular path of religious commitment loses its power, connections to loved ones are severed by illness, death. History, our times, our individual lives educate us to sustain only guarded optimisms, skeptical faith. And yet . . .

That "and yet" informs my efforts here and in the essays that follow. We possess the power to forge connections across time. In our blackest moments, we may read final loss. Yet the adventure of tracing connections, discovering links, rediscovering meaning can yield surprise and discovery for even the most dubious.

I compose this account with the hope, if not belief, that tracing the large arc of my musical life with its unpredictable, tangled strands, its involvement in worlds often now perceived as quaint or passé may yield insight about the profound and saving significance that making music has conferred on that life.

Although strange relations permeate the story, I hope, as well, that the effort to compose them may ultimately illumine their integral life-nourishing harmony.

A Grace Note

Cristofori's great invention worked no small miracle: shrank impossible distances, gave voice to another language, created a meeting in music, made us briefly one.

August 1967, Germany. Late afternoon. I am traveling in a Volkswagen with a friend of many years. After a long and distinguished career as an Ursuline nun, she has, like me, recently left off the habit of the Order. When I shed my black and white the previous April, I longed to visit one place: Salzburg. The name spells music. But how? My close friend Margaret, twenty years older, grasped the depth of my longing and agreed to go with me.

So here we are in the summer of 1967, navigating along a road lined by dense woods, in a new country. I'm in my fourth month of negotiating the great wide world in color, and I love it. In Wiesbaden I've just bought a fuschia sweater set with fake pearl buttons: daring.

I owe this trip to Grandpa, who years ago left me two thousand dollars in his will. Certain I would spend the rest of my life as an Ursuline, I had left this in my own will to the Order. Now I have left, and the Order has returned that two thousand dollars. Onward to Salzburg. Thank you, Grandpa.

First, though, we head to Michelstadt, a village in the heart of the Odenwald. Margaret has promised to try to find the mother and sisters of her nephew's German war bride. So, maps in hand, we drive over winding roads — avoiding the terrifying Autobahn — through tiny villages, past farms, asking directions in halting German, and finally wind up on a long low hill looking toward the church steeple of Michelstadt.

Behind a low stone wall, we arrive at a small square stone house with a steep red-tiled roof. We knock gently. Wait. A door slowly opens. From behind rimless glasses a tall thin white-haired woman in a plain blue cotton dress peers at us. Then, as if remembering that we might arrive, she smiles shyly. "Come in."

Awkward greetings, explanations in hesitant German, we soon gather about a table for hearty food: sliced meat, abundant potatoes. Talk is slow. Our hostess seems elderly, frail, with shaky hands. Her other daughter — not the one married to Margaret's nephew — lives with her mother. She is tall, slim, and bony. Clearly, the mother would like to chat if she knew more English. We are all slowly piecing it together — war, love affair, troubled loyalties, departure for America. The loss. Photos and polite talk are soon spent.

Silence. It lines the room. What can they ask us newly sprung nuns. No statues of Mary or Joseph here, no crucifix, no long thin face of Pope Pius XII looking at us. What do we know about Germany in 1967? What do they know about the United States? Vietnam is hardly a topic. Black power? Cross that one off. The riots plaguing American cities? Supreme Court deliberations on interracial marriage? We are far from home, in a strange new world that has survived more than bombs. Do the Beatles sing here too?

Silence. Too early to politely say good night. In one corner stands a dark heavy-looking upright piano, intricate carving along its sides.

Margaret eyes me. She mentions that I play.

"*Bitte*?"

How well I know this moment. Would you play something for us?

Except for two brief chances to accompany nuns' cantatas, I have officially touched no piano for thirteen years. My assigned keyboard was organ, my assigned repertoire liturgical.

Eyes on me. How can I say no?

Hesitant, I approach the piano, lift the top, see keys intact, turn to open the piano bench. What can I find? I have little in memory, know nothing of German lieder. "Tea for Two" won't cut it here. Nor "Sentimental Journey," still probably in my fingers. Edges of worn sheet music stare at me. Carefully, I leaf through the pile. Ah, Beethoven, "Sonata Pathétique." Maybe. There it is, the opening chord, the grand C minor. A blip of familiarity springs up within me. They are quiet, still at the dinner table, expectant.

I set my hands on the keyboard. Easy action. Pedals still work. Tuning just okay. I think I can do this.

Con brio does not apply here, but the second movement, hard to kill despite efforts of eager young pianists — ah, this does sing. That comforting word — *adagio*. And somehow I make it through the dazzling third movement.

In those minutes at the keyboard, I felt something release from me, an inner shadow I could not even now name. At the dinner table something almost tangible seems to have shifted. The mother's worn face holds a tentative smile; the daughter has reached over to hold the back of her mother's hand. Margaret looks relieved, more relaxed. Words are few but warm, grateful. Something fresh breathes around the room.

They were distant kin who had gone beyond speech, had nothing left to say, enclosed in a room. I was a visitor with no real connection. Jane Austen knew such rooms.

Beethoven saved us. He knew plenty about problems with communication, that lonely man. I played every repeat. The notes found my fingers, the sounds found my heart. I had studied this in seventh grade, with Professor Bonn. I turned eleven that year. Now I am thirty-five. Life surprises.

Afterward, through halting English with dictionary aid, we learn that the daughter who went off to America had played this piano. Now it sits there, mute monument to earlier good times, stolid memorial to lost harmonies.

Again, via Beethoven's hungering musical imagination, black marks on yellowing pages yielded their codes to my fingers, and Cristofori's great invention worked no small miracle: shrank impossible distances, gave voice to another language, created a meeting in music, made us briefly one.

Of the music we later heard in Salzburg I remember nothing.

This tiny ornament of our trip still sings in memory.

Six Bagatelles for Dancers

The band starts to play. The familiar itch consumes you. Your shiny black shoes move in time beneath the table. You glance at your mother, who, you can tell, is feeling the same urge. In contrast to your brother, now embarrassingly tall and pimpled, you have excelled at dancing school and long to put it to the test in public. You want to show off.

ONE: LEARNING THE STEPS
Time: Any Friday Afternoon or Evening between September and June, 1940–46
Place: Waterbury, Connecticut

Waterbury, Connecticut, is a town distinguished by a high percentage of Roman Catholics, largely second-generation immigrant factory workers now coalesced into strong ethnic communities, and a corresponding abundance of debt-ridden churches in sections of town serving Irish, French, Italian, Polish, Lithuanian, and German parishioners. By contrast, the fewer Protestant churches tend to be handsome in gray stone or gleaming white clapboard, and exhibit tenderly cared for landscapes beneath their splendid weather-vane-topped spires.

At the center of the large downtown green, a tall flag pole waves the Stars and Stripes high above a circle of seasonal flowers and various lollers-about relaxing on park benches here and there. To one side of the green, just across West Main Street, a large handsome Roman Catholic Romanesque church, the Immaculate Conception, holds its high gold doors open toward the green, the flag, the loiterers. If debt troubles this magnificent church, it certainly does not show. At the far end of the green, quietly elegant, stands St. John's Episcopal Church, stunning in its gray stone, doors locked except on Sunday.

In my study today hangs a poster showing Waterbury's dashing Fife and Drum Corps proudly strutting in red, white, and blue Revolutionary garb in front of St. John's. The banner flying alongside their U.S. flag identifies Mattatuck Fife and Drum Band, since 1767, the oldest fife and drum corps continuously operating in the country. Just visible behind them, on a little grass island near the church, stands the Soldier's Monument, tribute to those fallen in battle. Thus did one artist choose to synthesize a vision of history, religion, music, and patriotism with local color in downtown Waterbury, Connecticut.

While the presence, location, and relative number of churches may seem far removed from the learning of basic dance steps, perhaps it is not, or at least was not in that time and that place.

Across Prospect Street, on the opposite corner from the Immaculate Conception Church — locally referred to as "The Immaculate" — the Hotel Elton faces the green. During my growing-up years, entering the side door from Prospect Street would bring you into a short hallway. Turn left, go up a few steps, and you will come upon a small ballroom.

Friday dancing classes for children take place in this ballroom with its highly polished floor and its rows of straight-backed chairs along either side. Lasting one hour, classes begin at four in the afternoon, after school dismissal. As early as third grade, children may begin lessons. Parents anxious that their young fry absorb socially acceptable formulas of dance, deportment, and social discourse send their children here at the cost of twenty-five dollars per annum. Tap dance is offered somewhere else in town, but despite the example of Donald O'Connor and Fred Astaire, tap seems, at least for my parents, to lack sufficient social promise. At Miss Slocum's, it's virtually guaranteed that by the end of grammar school, your child will know the proper thing to do in a given social situation, whether or not she chooses to do it.

Just outside the ballroom, down a few steps and to the left, a cloakroom with racks of hangers and space for boots bustles with activity on Friday afternoon and evening as children are delivered by parents. Only at the final reception will parents be permitted to trip the light fantastic and survive a twirl with their own small fry or other prepubescent offspring. On that evening, niceties of "cutting in" and exchanging partners will be executed in an atmosphere at once cordial and reassuring.

For now, the task is to learn the steps.

As they shed their wraps, children laugh and talk and push and shove, bursting with end-of-school-week energy. Little girls display short dresses of velvet, cotton, and taffeta, white socks, and gleaming patent leather Mary Janes. The boys sport dark blue suits (short pants or long, depending on age and height), dark shoes and socks (high for those in shorts), white shirts, and ties. When the girls turn eleven or twelve and move into the after-supper class, they will wear stockings with low pumps; all the boys will graduate to long pants. White cotton gloves, it seems, transcend age or gender. Spanking fresh each week, they protect against sweating palms and are rarely forgotten.

As children mill about near the cloakroom waiting for the hour of their class, the first hurdle looms: partnering. Who will ask you to walk in with him? Jack Hutchinson, who bounces in the polka? Chubby Tuttle, who hops but is a good kid? Jerry Post, whose hands sweat through his gloves? Pee Wee Johnson, whose head scrapes your nose? Or, unasked this week, will you have to find a partner among the other stranded girls, preserve face, and walk in smiling?

"Walking in" is a big deal, a nerve-wracking liminal experience. It involves standing silently in line with the boy who has asked you to walk in with him, then going up the stairs together and into the ballroom where, just inside the doorway, you will be graciously greeted by the teacher, Miss Benita Virginia Slocum, and her assistants, Miss Coffee and Mrs. Arnold. By this time, your escort of the moment, be he four or five feet tall, has made sure he knows your name. He takes your gloved hand in his gloved hand and holds you forth to introduce you to Miss Slocum, who perfectly well knows who you are. She greets you both by name, he bows slightly, you curtsy, he turns away and leads you to a chair along the sidelines of the ballroom, then sits down beside you. Even at this stage, he has learned to see his partner off the dance floor and back to her place. No cheese is ever to be left standing alone at Miss Slocum's Dancing School.

You both sit with ankles crossed, hands on lap, until all the children have taken their places along the side of the ballroom, hands on laps, ankles crossed. In this orderly cosmos, attention deficit disorder and hyperactivity seem nonexistent; nudging, shoving, whispering, squirming were cast off with coats and boots in the cloakroom outside.

During this entrance ritual, at the far end of the ballroom on a slightly raised stage, Mrs. Larkin sits erect at the small cream-colored upright piano, playing something steadily rhythmic — one, two, three, four — to encourage the line of children forward for introductions.

You try to sit still, not your greatest talent. The piano's emphatic rhythms zap through you, tingle your feet as you sit there struggling not to twitch.

When the last young lady has taken her seat, Miss Slocum comes to the center of the room in her long salmon-colored gown and her dancing shoes. She faces you all, pleasant, a bit grave. "Good evening, girls and boys. Tonight we will begin with a review of the waltz. Please stand."

Miss Slocum, was she sixty, seventy, even eighty? Her face merges now with the face of Everywoman over sixty. But her dress, her stance, her manner, her firm steady courtesy, her patience — that remains seared in memory. Miss Slocum's hair was decidedly not white but colored a mousy brown and curled. She always wore a long dress with long sleeves, her feet and ankles exposed so you could watch and learn from them. Each Friday a large corsage decorated her left shoulder. She wore a hearing aid that sent a thin dark cord down behind the collar of her dress. She spoke clearly, but never raised her voice. I now know, from the article that *Life* magazine ran on that dancing school in 1945, that she was then seventy-seven and had been teaching dancing and deportment for fifty-four years.

You rise, take your places in lines on the floor, girls standing in front of boys, all facing Miss Slocum, waiting for her demonstration. The girls will first learn the boys' parts: waltz, fox trot, polka, or, later, rhumba, tango, Lindy hop, conga. Like all effective teachers, Miss Slocum breaks down the dance into clear formulas for the feet. After the basic steps have been mastered, the girls will practice them in reverse, with imaginary partners. Finally will come the moment when she pairs boys and girls and the truth will out: who can lead, who can follow, whose feet spring, whose feet drag.

For now, as Mrs. Larkin plays an unmistakable waltz, each child will follow Miss Slocum's elegant salmon-colored back, her trim ankles. Effortlessly, she demonstrates the first steps. She clacks her clacker and every child holds white gloved hands up, elbows bent, as he or she imitates those teaching shoes.

Dancing class has begun.

So it goes for six years. And while you are in those classes, the significance of whether you attend a stone church or a debt-ridden Roman Catholic church, whether you attend a small parochial school or a select private school, whether you live at the bottom of the hill, the top of the hill, or outside town in the rolling green Connecticut countryside and keep horses, begins to sink in. By eighth grade you understand that a chasm of class, custom, religious practice, inherited privilege, and expectation separates your own Irish-Catholic middle-class family from "The Four Hundred," the established Yankee residents of Waterbury, Connecticut, and environs, the families that own the factories.

Even so, you have had the advantage of learning the basic steps. And there is no telling when they may come in handy, where they may lead.

Two: On the Roof
Time: March 1943
Place: The Hotel New Yorker, Manhattan

Newsreels persistently remind that "our boys" are being killed or wounded "Over There." "When Johnny Comes Marching Home Again," "Anchors Away, My Boys," and Kate Smith's "God Bless America" echo in your head as Frank Sinatra and Donald O'Connor tap their way in uniform across the big screen at Loew's Poli Theatre on Saturday afternoons.

For Waterbury, Brass Center of the World, the war effort has special meaning. Scovill, American Brass, Chase Brass and Copper — their shops teem with defense workers, many of them women, churning out bullets, brass buttons, and fodder for the defense industry. Blackout curtains have been hung around town, and during air raid drills, fathers and uncles prowl neighborhoods to check that no light shows through the fissures of that darkened world.

Yet light finds its fissure and dazzles an eleven-year-old moving with her brother and parents through a wilderness of neon, crowds, sirens, horns, shouts, and murmurs — even in wartime, Manhattan is Manhattan. You and your mother knit socks for "the boys." You and your brother crush aluminum cans. Your dad finds ways to get extra ration books. The War, however, touches you largely through pictures and voices: Van Johnson stunning in uniform, Vera Lynn singing patriotism, Lowell Thomas crooning the evening news, an extra Hail Holy Queen each morning at school for "our boys" fighting in this valley of tears.

This is no valley of tears. Here you are, in the embrace of parents who have brought you to experience the City. You've seen *Oklahoma* and watched Ralph Edwards' radio show, *Truth or Consequences*. At *Hellzapoppin*, Olsen and Johnson actually brought you up on stage. All of that was prelude to this cool Friday evening in downtown Manhattan. Your father and mother have decided to bring you and your thirteen-year-old brother to the Starlight Roof. You wear a maroon velvet dress with a lace collar, flesh-colored nylons with seams up the back, and Mary Janes with T-straps. Getting ready in your room at the New Yorker Hotel, your mother curled your hair with the curling iron, carefully slipping a comb between the heat and your scalp as she wrapped each bunch of hair around the iron. You watched her curl her eyelashes with that funny metal object she carries for special occasions.

Nothing of the food, the drink, the light talk of that evening now remains. What sticks is the generalized heady aura of being out in Manhattan with your parents and sitting at a table covered by a thick white tablecloth, surrounded by conversational murmur and the clinking of glasses, right next to the crowded dance floor . . . and longing to be out there.

The band starts to play. The familiar itch consumes you. Your shiny black shoes move in time beneath the table. You glance at your mother, who, you can tell, is feeling the same urge. In contrast to your brother, now embarrassingly tall and pimpled, you have excelled at dancing school and long to put it to the test in public. You want to show off. You look at your father. You know he is not feeling well, but he is your only hope. "Would you like to dance?" he finally says. Or perhaps your mother leaned over and whispered to him, "Bill, take her out to the dance floor."

He does like to show you off, his only daughter. You both get up, head for the dance floor as the band starts a waltz. One two three, one two three. It invades your sinews, your muscles, your bones, zings through you as you rise to the balls of your feet, ready. You know how to follow your partner as he leads you through a turn and oh, finally, sometimes into a dip at the very end.

Your dad's stomach grazes you; your head comes to his shoulder. The trouble is . . . you don't dance. He has this odd way of just moving forward. Later you will hear it called the two step. It is totally unsatisfying. Why can't he feel the rhythm and follow it; why can't he at least do a box step? No, just forward and then forward, a bit like walking, sometimes a chassée, only you can never tell just when he will stick one in.

Three of the six years he has been given to live have already passed. You know this. Your home is kept quiet. Afternoons when he gets home from work at the Connecticut Light & Power Co., he often rests before dinner. One day not too long ago when you were with him in the living room, helping him turn the key that lifts the heavy weights on the grandmother clock, he said, "Who's going to do this when I kick the bucket?" Heart sinking you rose to the occasion and told him you would. Years later you will interpret this memorable New York excursion as his attempt to outwit time, now rather than later. There will be no later.

He pushes you forward through the other dancers for a bit, then has to stop. You both go back to the table. No doubt your face makes it clear that although you have danced, you haven't really danced. You're trying to be good; after all this is a special trip. But even if your father doesn't know how to dance, you do.

After a few moments, a man from a neighboring table, comes over to speak to your parents. "I wonder, would you mind if I danced with your daughter?"

You're ready to leap up from the table, hit the dance floor, execute a dazzling dip. You'd like to be June Allyson, Judy Garland, Ginger Rogers all wrapped up into one. Oh, for the chance to show what you have so aptly learned. (On other occasions, you also long to be Jennifer Jones in *The Song of Bernadette* — who, regrettably, didn't dance.)

Mr. Ruff introduces himself to you and pulls out your chair. Unfazed, nervously happy, you feel his hand on your elbow piloting you to the dance floor. Ah, bliss, it's instantly clear: he can dance. You can follow. He can lead. And not only does he know the box step and the turn, he can also maneuver you into the conversational, which you've recently learned. Oh, this is heaven. And a little hesitation when he senses it in the music. Totally in command, Mr. Ruff moves you through the steps on the dance floor to the strains of some song you cannot now name. For a few little twirls under his arm, he pushes you through and is there to catch you on the return. At the end, oh joy, he leads you into a dip. For the first time, a strong arm holds you steady instead of the little boy arm, which always threatens to let you go kerplunk.

And then it is over.

The night fades. The hotel, the size of the rooms, the neon names on Broadway — all of it fades. There remains one golden moment on the dance floor.

Mr. Ruff.

He was a stranger. You were a little girl dressed up and out with your parents and brother for a big evening. He observed the forms of courtesy. It worked. He led you through the dance. You knew what to do. Your steps followed his; together you moved in time to the music. He returned you to the table, to your family, and left you feeling accomplished, happy, noticed, admired.

You felt the joy of finding a suitable partner for the dance.

What fun for an eleven-year-old girl in the midst of World War II, out for an evening in Manhattan with a father who would die two years later, a brother who would see his own military service and later die too young, a mother who would never, into her nineties, lose her ability to dance.

THREE: LEARNING THE STEPS PAID OFF
Time: Late May 1964
Place: The World's Fair,
Flushing Meadows, New York

The driver wedges the station wagon between a Chrysler and a maroon Buick, and six figures climb out clothed in black to the ankles, their faces framed by starched white headdresses. Each sister carries a small paper bag with a peanut butter sandwich, two cookies, and a small carton of apple juice inside. Deep in each underskirt pocket, next to the rosary case, lies a folded five dollar bill.

The day glows. A high bright sun beats down on their covered heads; a welcome breeze ruffles veils. High domes; spires; cubes of plastic, cement, and steel; and puffy white clouds dot the sky, a blue sky today. Thank God for the breeze, for it is hot, and black serge does not breathe.

Their two-dollar entrance fee paid by the senior sister, the six nuns head for the Unisphere, a huge glittering globe with stainless steel rings, symbol of this year's World's Fair.

Water, water everywhere — lakes, lagoons, reflecting pools, fountains — this make-believe world is awash in water. At the base of the Unisphere, a reflecting pool receives the tossed coins of passersby, hopes tossed for progress, tossed toward a future without pain, without shadow. Coins of hope. The nuns have no coins to throw away.

Children with ice cream dripping from their mouths run by, parents at the chase. The smell of pizza floats on the air, enough to make any abstemious nun's mouth water. Grown-ups stream past balancing Belgian waffles topped with strawberries and whipped cream as children tug at their hands. In the International Section, sixty-six countries are officially represented. Flags snap brilliant rainbows in the wind: New York, New Jersey, Wisconsin, Pakistan, Sweden, France, the world.

The Swiss Sky Ride screams above you. Everyone seems to

be wearing yellow General Electric buttons proclaiming, "I Have Seen the Future." As you notice the buttons, a long buried memory pops up: the trip to the World's Fair in 1939 with your parents and brother. The four of you stood mesmerized before General Motors' Futurama, fascinated by sleek automobiles racing around landscaped highways, through tunnels, over bridges. And here you are now, twenty-five years later, plunk inside that Futurama. You traveled a landscaped highway to get here, zoomed beneath tunnels, across bridges in a sleek automobile. You are covered in black and white, veiled. Who could have seen this future? Yet "I Have Seen the Future" buttons continue to sell.

Do we ever willingly dispense with illusion?

Does the future never lose its lure?

Straight ahead, the Vatican Pavilion, its gold roof agleam. To look at it hurts the eyes.

First, you all must locate the Pietà. If Mary and her son had not made this trip to Flushing Meadows, neither would you. Seeing her tops the official list of things to do. After the Vatican Pavilion, you will be freed to roam for several hours before returning to the parking lot, climbing into the van, heading back to your cloistered convent in New Rochelle. A rare event, this, for semi-cloistered nuns who are allowed out only for purposes of health or education. Some higher power has judged the World's Fair educational. And you have your own secret plan.

Pinkerton men guard the doorway to the Vatican Pavilion. "They wanted to dress the Pinkerton men like Swiss Guard," remarks one nun as you all board the conveyor belt that will carry you slowly past the Mother and her Son. "Rome was smart enough to say no."

You cannot summon a reply. Part of you wants to see the Pietà. If not now, when?

Hot expectant humans breathe around you. The tall clergyman beside you in a gray suit with a Roman collar looks pinched, as if behind that cloth secret pain simmers. Ahead of you, a small stocky woman, her long blonde curls pulled back by a knotted cowboy-style kerchief, her purple high heels fairly tottering as she clutches the rail, turns to you, eyes aglow. "I'm so excited, Sister," she whispers. "This is what I came to see. I came all the way from Wyoming."

What did you go into the desert to see? A reed shaken in the wind?

The conveyor belt moves slowly, like a department store escalator propelled by an outside power, headed this time not for Ladies Ready-to-Wear but for the Lady herself.

Bulletproof Lucite will protect viewers as they look into the large blue velour grotto. Monks from somewhere can be heard chanting the Solemn Salve Regina. *Ad te suspiramus, gementes et flentes in hac lacrimarum valle.* You think: what a farce. Thomas Merton should see this. Could Trappists in backwoods Kentucky in their sweat-drenched cowls guess what use their sublime prayer would be put to?

The conveyor belt inches out of the wings toward the center. Suddenly, it shudders.

Et Jesum, benedictum fructrum ventris tui.

There she is. Her serene face inclines over the body of her dead son.

What did you go into the desert to see?

Fifty spotlights beaming down on the figure of Mary and her dead son... *nobis post hoc exsilium ostende* ... fake votive candles and half-watt blue lights, four hundred of them, twinkling to create a phony atmosphere of peace, of prayer, of what?

You stop for a moment directly in front of the virgin, the mother. And there, before that sublime form, so simple, so pure, your mind finally grows still. Pure grief in the cold embrace of white Carrara marble.

Then ... gone.

The belt jiggles along.

"Wasn't she beautiful?" whispers the small woman, pressing against you.

How do you isolate such a moment from its context? How do you learn to ignore implication? *Unless you become as little children you cannot enter the kingdom of heaven.* Becoming as little children itself holds too much implication.

One by one you step off the conveyor belt and move en masse into the center of the pavilion where Cardinal Spellman's stamp and coin collection is on view. Nuns of every stripe and color surround you, habits in various stages of reconstruction and deconstruction: ankle length, calf length, knee length, tones of navy blue and gray, modest, unstylish, headdresses pared down to reveal hair, clumps of laced black oxfords beside which your black loafers (no pennies) look positively daring. Cloistered eyes stare at the display on Catholic schools. Catholic schools make a twenty-two billion dollar contribution to the American economy. In these days of Vatican II, you've been wondering about that contribution, for no assertion about the Church in America or, for that matter, in the world now seems clear or simple, devoid of context, of implication. Nearby, slide boxes demonstrate the life of the church and, for the Eucharist, include a glossy close-up of grapes, a loaf of Jewish rye, a wine glass, a basket of rolls.

Does a figure with a whip wait just beyond the door to the Vatican Pavilion?

Release will come.

Live rhythms will displace canned monks, real dancing subsume frozen grief. You have a secret. You have set it up in advance with a sympathetic nun companion — for nuns still must travel in twos. You will ditch the others and make your way to the Spanish Pavilion.

As crowds ooze away from displays and out the door, two nuns drift off to sit in the giant floating egg, a feature of I.B.M. Two others want to experience the picture phone. You are all to meet by the Unisphere at five o'clock. Sister Maura, true friend, stays with you.

You both move quickly on ahead, threading the crowd, and finally pass through the huge grilled door of the Spanish Pavilion into space, open space, blooming with the color of hundreds of flowers, but it's not so much color as the sense of spaciousness itself that meets you head on, as if suddenly the world opened, as if somehow space itself could offer you the gift of inner freedom. You are gloriously free of the crowded, noisy, sweaty, exhilarating streets of the World's Fair outside this enclosure. Seclusion strokes your soul, hushes its murmurs, a different kind of air brushes your starch-framed cheek. Many years later, watching prisoners emerge from dungeon darkness in Beethoven's *Fidelio*, dark ragged figures slowly reaching for light, for air, breathing first in quiet wonder, their voices gradually swelling in their glorious hymn to air:

> *O welche Lust! In freier Luft*
> *den Atem leicht zu heben!*
> *Nur hier, nur hier ist Leben,*
> *der Kerker eine Gruft.*
> *Sprecht leise, haltet euch zurück!*
> *Wir sind belauscht mit Ohr und Blick.*

You will momentarily leave the Seattle Opera House and return to this transforming moment in the courtyard of the Spanish Pavilion when you yourself seemed to breathe in a new elixir created by space, as if a sudden openness supplied new life to your spirit, to your soul.

> O what joy in the open air
> To breathe with ease!
> Only here, only here is life,
> the prison a tomb.
> Speak softly, restrain yourselves!
> We are overheard by ears and eyes.

Together you now hurry by Turcios's murals, subdued grays, blacks, tans, and white tones narrating Spanish discovery and conquest, understated images of power perfectly integrated with the architecture of this wondrous pavilion. You climb the massive stairway past white stucco walls and move through geranium-crowded courtyards to the exhibitions. You want to pause everywhere as you pass through museum alcoves and the gallery of Old Masters; you have never been to Europe and have no hope of going there.

Guitars throb. You hurry past a statue of Junípero Serra. There isn't time to stop and gawk. You have tickets. A truly astonishing fact. How would you have tickets when religious poverty demands that all household money be controlled by the superior? A superior who, you are perfectly clear, would never, even for educational reasons, send you to a show. These tickets were not distributed by your superior. In fact, she knows nothing about them. Thanks to the discreet generosity of a friend on the outside, you and your friend on the inside are about to have a great, illicit treat. Your pulse throbs in anticipation.

Finally, the theater.

And now it begins. On the large stage, the perfect dialogue of body and mind. Guitars weep and cry their subtle rhythms, growing, growing. Feet stamp, elbows bend, knees flicker, layers of ruffled hemlines wave. You sit in the dark, mesmerized. What is this sinuous geometry of the body that gathers into itself so many moods — anger, fear, passion, betrayal, jealousy — dispersing them through the bend of an elbow, the tension of a knee? The gentle, supple, curving arms, the revolving wrists, the swiveling hips, the eloquent hands of this woman who dances with a shawl as if it were a partner, her speaking fingers part of the dance. And the slow, controlled movement of the tall, slim man in his skin-tight black pants, his dark hat and ruffled shirt, as he twirls, bows, advances, stands aside, surveys, and stretches into the turn and stamp of a shiny black boot. You want to be inside those orange ruffles, make them dip; you want to learn how to manage the intricate clicks of those black heels, how to swirl a shawl as if it were a partner; you want to know how to tease with long slender legs, with which you, unfortunately, have not been blessed. How is it possible to combine such elaborate showiness with such interiority? How can subtle abstraction be embodied in such austere, disciplined body gestures? Here, in the gorgeous building simulating the courtyards of Castille, the filigreed palaces of Andalusia, you are no longer, for one hour, held in a vise of white starch and covered by a long black skirt with no ruffles. You are elsewhere.

You are, in fact, the only nuns in the theater.

You want to stay, see it again, delay the moment of leaving.

The images, the rhythm, the sustained pauses, the gorgeous stately moves, the nimble ankles. The wonderful click click and stamp of those marvelous black shoes. The slowly weaving arms of the dancers, the graceful wrists, the perfectly calibrated invitation and delay, the gracious, teasing dialogue of man and woman, seducer and seduced, the seen and the ignored, heel and toe, body and mind. Flamenco.

Back, then, to the Unisphere.

Years later, many years later, you will see flamenco dancing again, up close enough to watch beads of sweat appear on the intense faces, and you will recognize, in the words of Federico García Lorca, the astonishing accomplishment of the flamenco dancer:

> The dancer's trembling heart must bring everything into harmony, from the tips of her shoes to the flutter of her eyelashes, from the ruffles of her dress to the incessant play of her fingers. Shipwrecked in a field of air, she must measure lines, silences, zigzags, and rapid curves with a sixth sense of aroma and geometry, without ever mistaking her terrain. In this she resembles the torero, whose heart must keep to the neck of the bull. Both of them face the same danger: he, death; and she, darkness.

She must fill a dead, gray space with a living, clear, trembling arabesque, one which can be vividly remembered. This is how she speaks, this is her tongue.[4]

FOUR: IN THE KITCHEN
Time: Noon on a September Day, 1982
Place: Sackville, New Brunswick, Canada,
Population: 3,000

It isn't the perfect ballroom, but the new floor works. We've finally gotten rid of the loathsome brown kitchen rug that displayed every speck of flour, and this new cushiony floor works for dancing. Besides, this isn't romantic or display dancing. It's fun dancing.

The theater is in a small town in New Brunswick, Canada, home of two stove foundries, a university, and a few other smaller enterprises. Tom, the older son, is in seventh grade at the one local elementary school. This is the era of bullies in the schoolyard. He can walk home from school for lunch. We live just a few blocks away.

I'm in the kitchen preparing a lunch for him and his dad, who also may arrive over the noon hour, walking home from the university, only five minutes away.

Last summer, at a family dance camp in Pointe-de-l'Église, Nova Scotia, a week of lessons in four types of social dancing — ballroom, folk, square, and Scottish — taught us, among many other things, the cha-cha. During this school year, my husband and I have guaranteed ourselves a weekly date: we drive to Moncton, the nearest city, where we drop Tom off for his tap lesson while we head for ballroom dance lessons at Club D'age D'or. The Spanish Pavilion this is not. Nor are we costumed in ruffles, shawls, skin-tight black pants, and snapping black heels. Nonetheless, we have found a fine teacher, Aurelle Belliveau, and weekly he puts us through newly learned paces doing the cha-cha, rhumba, waltz, foxtrot. We dance international style now, which differs from the beginnings we made at an Elks Club in McMinnville, Oregon, when we were on leave there last academic year. The quickstep, dazzling to behold and difficult to execute, challenges us. Dance camp last summer has enlarged our repertoire of steps and heightened our confidence. Each evening the kids, who had been in their own dance classes during the day, had a chance to join the larger party in the school gym where we all danced, about 150 strong, whatever we'd been drilling that day.

Executions of the jive were sometimes a wonder to witness — that tossing and twirling and complicated messaging back and forth between partners, the sheer energetic fun of it.

Now we are back home, dance camp over, school year begun. The urge to move a body in rhythm to music hasn't quite succumbed to winter inertia. And so, on some days shortly after noon, Tom arrives. I have the music on. He's keen for the jive and cha-cha. We hit it, on the cushion floor, usually the jive, for then he gets to push his mother around: twirl me, under his arm, out from him, wind up, unwind, all with a certain glee at his mastery. The younger bones are more fluid, and when we do the cha-cha, his hips are looser, while mine say I am now a mother. He has a terrific sense of rhythm.

Round and round we go in the kitchen, sandwiches waiting as we narrowly avoid bumping counters or stove. This ballroom is much too small. Giggles set in as he speeds things up, throws me around; I grow short-winded, breathless, cry for him to stop, and still he leads on and on until I drop to the floor laughing hysterically.

When his dad comes in he finds me rolling on the floor, breathless.

Sandwiches come after.

The walk to school comes after.

Facing bullies comes after.

Classes in French immersion come after. Math, social

studies, English, science — all comes after the dance. Composing a new story comes after. Returning to face university students comes after.

What is this dancing?

It's an interlude from life, something light, something quick, something that leaves us breathlessly laughing. A reprieve. A move away from shadows.

A far cry from Miss Slocum, this. A farther cry, yet, from a nun sitting in the Spanish Pavilion at the World's Fair, throbbing to the beat, longing to dance.

Farther still from a fifth-grade little girl anxious to be on the dance floor and prove herself able to keep step with the gentleman from the next table who asks her to dance. The Starlight Roof? That was another country.

These are crevices in time, that's all.

Discern the crevice. Inhabit it while you can.

Time: Eight O'Clock on a Spring Evening, 2003.

Place: Salem, Oregon.

Now all these years later, twenty-one of them, and no longer living in Canada, no longer with children at home, we live on Mill Creek in Salem, showers-with-sunny-breaks Oregon. We decided one evening last spring to invite new neighbors from across the creek for dinner. We invited our other nearby neighbors on this side of the creek, as well, to join us for a potluck.

Around the dinner table by candlelight, near the framed Gregorian chant that celebrates *Hodie nata est*, our new neighbors, Kate and Lee, seemed to be enjoying this return to a neighborhood Kate had known as a child. In their return, they are starting a new life.

Toward the end of the meal, Kate lifted her head and looked around the table: "I have a confession to make," she said in a quiet voice.

Ears pricked up. Forks were set down.

She looked at me and then at my husband as if sizing up both us and the moment.

"I looked over the other night and the light was on in your kitchen," she said. During spring and the long summer, trees shade both sides of the creek, but now our large sycamore was still pretty bare. "I looked over to see if you'd wave to me," she went on, for occasionally we've waved at each other through our respective kitchen windows when the trees are bare and we putter about preparing dinner. "I couldn't see you," she said. "But then I saw something moving and I watched. It was the two of you in the kitchen," she said with a slight hesitation, "and you seemed to be hugging."

No one was eating.

"I watched. Then I saw that you were moving as you hugged. You were dancing. I could see you holding one another, moving around, and I just stood there and watched. I didn't want it to stop. It was beautiful."

FIVE: IN THE LIVING ROOM
Time: Any Afternoon between 1948 and 1954
Place: A Six-Room Apartment, Buckingham Street, Waterbury, Connecticut

Two years after my father's death, my mother sold the big house that could accommodate both my brother's extensive drum set and my Chickering piano in one end of the living room, and we moved to an apartment. I was then a sophomore in high school, and my mother remained in this apartment for years after I entered the convent. The living room in this apartment was not very large, but it could hold two dancers if they kept their steps small. This smaller living room preserved the essentials: the Chickering, three easy chairs, fireplace with mantel that held several knickknacks, couch Mother could sleep on when relatives arrived and we needed more sleeping space. The drums were gone. My brother was off at boarding school.

My mother loved to dance.

For seventeen years she was married to a man with minimal sense of rhythm, still less of tune, the apex of whose musical outlet occurred when, on rare occasions, he would be driving us all home from somewhere on a Sunday, perhaps a visit to relatives in Litchfield, and he would break into "Should auld acquaintance be forgot . . ." Then he would stop; that was it.

For her part, Mother would now and then break into the first bars of "He's just my Bill," for him.

Ours was not, however, a singing household. I consider that a loss.

We had 78s that featured "The Charleston! The Charleston! Made in Carolina!" and now, decades past her flapper days but still nimble, my mother set herself to teach me the Charleston. These were my high school years when monthly CYO dances in the auditorium at Waterbury Catholic High School held little demand for the Charleston. Boys with crew cuts and leather jackets cruised about the crowded dance floor, hesitant to actually dance, as nuns watched from the sidelines.

Now and then, when Mother had come home from the work she returned to after she lost dad and I had finished with all my after-school music activities and had not begun to crack the pile of books waiting for me on the desk, we would dance. I would have changed from my navy blue serge uniform and long sleeved white cotton blouse into dungarees and T-shirt.

We would put on a record, face each other in the living room on the rug with its patterns of rose and black and dull green against a neutral gray. The record would blare: "The Charleston! The Charleston! Made in Carolina!" and she would break into it. Bothered by feet that sometimes kept her awake at night, she now abstained from spike heels and strove to make her peace with detested, low-heeled, black lace oxfords.

So there we would be, I in bare feet, she in sensible shoes, facing one another, piano in one corner, sofa against the other wall, a chair or two moved out of our way, and above the fireplace on the mantel were statues of two gracious ladies draped in pastel colors who always seemed to suggest the kind of elegance my mother longed for.

We were anything but elegant: knees in, knees out, hands out, then back in to cross in front, as we bent slightly forward, turned heels inward, then toes inward, and went to it. No dangling pearls on mom now, no slim glittery flapper dress as I'd seen in old photos of an earlier time. Instead, a pique house dress, or seersucker, or in winter, perhaps a matching sweater and skirt, toned to whatever the colors were that year. Heels in, toes out, then reverse, and now, the little touch you don't always see: bend the knees, cross the hands, keep the feet moving, cross and re-cross on the knees as you bend forward. Now do the kick out, as you swing arms across each other in front of you.

Over and over until the record stopped, and then we would collapse on the sofa or easy chair, breathless, exhilarated.

Back then to what was for supper, the homework at the desk, the Latin, the math, the ordinary high school stuff.

And for Mother, back to sustaining the life of a woman early widowed, longing for style and comfort, back now to work to support and educate two growing children.

The dancing moment, though, leaps full-blown into memory. The living room became a room of living, full of music and movement, energy, as if to say to the framed picture of my father dominating the wall — and in later years of my dead brother next to but slightly below him: "We can still dance, Bill. We're having a ball." Life goes on . . . beyond the pictures of graduation, of uncles and aunts gathered for ritual holidays, of our dead grandmother from Ireland, and all the moments that suggest time has stopped.

Is it, then, that time stops while you dance? Or is it really a different kind of time?

That may be closer to it. You were in the enchanted crevice, protected from whatever preys, consumes, threatens, invades, destroys. For the length of a Charleston, you were safe, dancing within a fissure of light.

Pure gift.

Six: In the Moment
Out of Time
Out of Place
What are the steps we need to learn?
And where can we learn them?

Despite images that Shakespeare puts before us to resolve his comedies, despite the glorious dances that Mozart and Gilbert and Sullivan offer us to round off tales of intrigue, disguise, infidelity, forgiveness, betrayal, mismatches re-matched, and impoverished heroes suddenly revealed as royal offspring, life offstage engages us only sometimes in its deeply comedic aspect.

Comedy offers the relief of steps laid out before us, steps the actors and actresses must themselves learn in order to arrive at the closing dance, to dramatize for their audience the possibility of resolution beyond tragedy.

As an image of life's consummate and passing joys, the dance prevails. When the Duke at the close of *The Marriage of Figaro* calls for the dance, we understand. Forgiveness triumphs, manipulation and disguise have achieved their goals: to instruct, to please, to lead to revelation, recognition, and the joy of happy partnering. Mozart and DaPonte have led us neither to Valhalla nor to Faust's eternal fire, but to a place of this world where, inside the dance, human earthly joy is caught and known to us, for a long moment before the final curtain falls.

My last bagatelle of the dance encompasses a small clear space, a circle of light set within a darker context.

The Odd Fellows Hall in Amherst, Nova Scotia, is a clapboard structure on La Planche Street. On Valentine's Day, 1987 — or 1986 or 1985 — that space was occupied by a dance for young people. That the precise date matters little suggests how imprecise are the standard markers for growing up, how unpredictable the cycles of maturing for a child who suffers from delayed development. Add to that unpredictability the vagaries of attention deficit disorder that entail a radical pull into the moment itself, as if one could tear that moment out of time's flow and climb inside it, devoid of context.

Knowing a goal and steps toward it offers a measure of security, a way of charting progress, achievement, within a given context. To find a partner whose steps may mesh creatively with yours, answering rather than duplicating your own, can entail many snags, delusions, and deceptions of hope. I know this path and rejoice in having found such a partner. Dancing — so beautiful in the Astaire mode, so joyful when Gene Kelly goes "Singin' in the Rain," so marvelous when Pegleg Clayton taps designs beyond our conceiving or Ruby Keeler shuffles off to Buffalo — conveys the artful deception that mastering steps is easy, that an arm will always be there to keep you from falling in a dip.

If, however, all steps are unclear, the goal simply not there, how then does one find a partner to share that unmarked floor? There are no elegant ankles to follow, no beat impelling you to snap your ruffles and click your heels, no regular music inviting you forward toward a gracious welcome into the ballroom of life. Thomas Mann's memorable figure, Tonio Kröger, seemed destined to stand fixed forever outside the dance. Can such a figure — in life, not fiction — experience sudden moments of shared rhythm, exhilaration, and ecstatic relief?

Yes. The human body is a wondrous thing, the brain even more so. And if one's circuitry differs, as in the case of our dancer here, and one's behavioral patterns cannot easily be read, nonetheless, it may happen in a given moment that something deep is revealed and shines out of the neural dark.

I have witnessed it.

This is the younger son, who danced for pennies in the ninth grade cafeteria until authorities intervened, trying to explain to him "implication." This is the same boy who expertly propelled confused older ladies through intricate square dance maneuvers at dance camp as the caller escalated complexity far past do-si-do. This is the boy who later, baffled to find himself adrift on the unmarked floor of adolescence (the very concept of "steps" distasteful, perhaps unfathomable), will seek release and attention on the tiny dance floor at a local bar-cum-club, until a phone call is made to parents. The word "exploitation" is used.

Nonetheless, here, on the small dance floor in the Odd Fellows Hall, at this special dance for variously disabled teenagers, our young man of fourteen, or fifteen, or sixteen, or perhaps twelve, finds his partner. Chauffeured by his parents, he has called for her at her home. This special event has required of him extra scrubbing, shaving, and dressing up. Running shoes, T-shirts, jeans have been left behind. In his pressed black trousers, dark shoes and socks, white long-sleeved shirt with tie, and his dad's blue and white striped sports jacket, he is looking even more handsome than usual.

Once arrived at the Odd Fellows Hall, the dancers check coats, turn away from parents and, as the music starts up — something loud, with a heavy beat — they head together to the dance floor, sharing space with twenty or thirty other young people.

They do not need to embrace one another. There seems to be no leading or following. Instead, something mysterious occurs almost immediately, a shared intuition about each other's movements, separate, yet together, she in her size two shoes, her ballerina-like red skirt with net showing underneath, her bright blue eyes, her freshly curled hair, he shining with excitement. Then, as the dancing intensifies, bit by bit, the jacket is shed, the strangling tie pulled loose, the shirt collar unbuttoned, the legs and hips grow so fluid, so graceful, the shirt springs from above the creased black trousers, the dark eyes grow brighter, the dark curly hair begins to glisten. Bones, sinews, ligaments, tendons, hands, arms, shoulders, knees, ankles, feet, synapses — one long elastic thread seems to join every part in a perfect dance, together, speaking to one another with their bodies, answering. No Hermes Pan needed to choreograph this; no Ruby Keeler shuffling off to Buffalo hovers dimly in sight. A cosmos separates our dancers from the world of gigue, courante, gavotte, minuet. Neither breakdancing nor the moonwalk touch this. This is their own creation, perfect improvising, rhythmic, daring, playful footwork, body movement, joyful in the moment, untroubled by misstep or mishap, unique, perfect.

For a time, in that drab setting, a spotlight of attention shines brightly on the couple. They inhabit that light, fully.

They execute a choreography of the chosen.

What their bodies do is stunning. You could wish for such abandon to the rhythm of the moment.

After this night, they will never see each other again.

Yet for now, the deep nourishing joy-giving now, they dance inside time, stretching it, shrinking it, according to their whim.

What is that other world out there where time is numbered on the clock by sequences of seconds, where responsibilities borne assume density in duration, where work replaces play and ought becomes norm? It is another world, the world of parents, non-dancers, distant, exiled. Outside the dance.

They have not seen the future. They need help reading the present.

Ours is a different world, our very own, inside the dance: safe, rhythmic, shared, its time unmeasured, its end unknown, unanticipated, unthought of. We can dance until the music stops. After the music of this evening, we need never meet again.

Time has shrunk to now. We are in it.

We are it.

This is my other son.

His dance is supreme, its steps known to him alone.

Beyond words.

I stand outside, watch.

And marvel.

LEARNING TO PLAY

Despite his meticulous and rigorous attention to details of technique, somehow what breathed through the lessons was always music, not mechanics. Had it not been so, I surely would have given it up.

Once a week, from second through eighth grade, I walked at the end of the school day from St. Margaret School up the long slope of Willow Street in Waterbury, Connecticut, past the hair salon, past the drugstore, grocery store, and fire station — always with two or three firemen relaxing on chairs out front — to my weekly music lesson with Professor John L. Bonn. After what felt like many blocks, Willow Street turned into Willow Extension, left businesses behind, and became residential: rows of large shaded frame houses, two or three stories, with awninged porches and flowering bushes out front.

Part way up the street, on the left, I came to the large gray house with its expansive porch. I'd ring the front doorbell and be greeted by Professor Bonn, or sometimes by the mysterious elderly woman who lived with him — Miss Pease, dressed always in black. Once she let me in, she would silently glide upstairs. That was all I ever knew of her.

Just inside the door a small waiting area had one wall covered with bookcases, two comfortable chairs, a floor lamp, and a table. Here I sat and waited until Professor Bonn appeared from upstairs or finished the lesson before mine in the adjoining room. From the bookcase I would locate my current book, search out my place marker, settle down, and begin to read.

When he finally ushered me into his large double living room plus studio with its fireplace, dark chairs, standing lamps, and two grand pianos at the far end, he would adjust the pile of yellow music books on the piano bench in front of the piano I was allowed to play. Each year he adjusted the height of the pile for my size.

In a cordial, encouraging, but somewhat formal atmosphere, he created an hour that was all about music, no social frills. He seemed ancient, Professor Bonn. His origins were mysterious. Germany, we thought. He was ugly. A big mole on his right cheek sprouted a hair. I didn't like to look at it. A tall man, always in a shiny dark suit, white shirt and tie, he walked with a slight stoop and his spotted hands trembled, except when he set them on the keyboard. At the parish High Mass on Sundays, he played the organ up in the balcony and sometimes sang parts of the Mass in his faint quavery voice.

As the lesson proceeded, on each piece of music his shaky hand would write the metronome marking I was to aim for during the next week's practice. Week after week he would move it up a notch. That, however, was a minor part of the lesson. Surely he knew that at home I avoided the metronome.

He would often write a chord's symbol above it — G7 for the dominant seventh, the small circle for the diminished, the plus sign for augmented, and so on. In that way, from very early on he trained me to look at notation as a key to something else, the harmonic structure, the chord progressions that those black notes signified. Though important, simply reading notes was never enough. He demonstrated how those patterns worked together, what they "said." He would play a dominant seventh chord "crying to go home," as he put it, then wait while I located the related tonic chord on the keyboard.

I now realize he was introducing me to a whole other language, its grammar, the meanings it could hold, and its rhetorical implications, though he never talked that way. He simply moved from one piece to another, along the way choosing samples of whatever seemed appropriate to my progress, interest, needs, talent, or indolence. This was all classical music, with substantial doses of Beethoven. I played only one Debussy that I recall, "Clair de Lune," but he occasionally lightened my programs with "Nola" or "Juba" or "Golliwog's Cakewalk." On my own, far away from Professor Bonn, I would hunt out sheet music for the day's popular songs and learn them. He resided far from the world of Sinatra.

I had no exposure to a traditional music series book. Instead, in a sense I had to make my own. For each week's lesson I had to write out the I–IV–V chords for a specific key in every inversion and then, at the lesson, demonstrate them on the piano. Over time I covered every key and wrote, as well, the appropriate root in the bass clef along with its chords. Later teachers would point out aspects of harmony in a piece, but never with such consistency, week by week, over so many years.

Touch — together we explored the different ways of touching a key and its effects. Chopin's students tell of his strategies to elicit as many kinds of sounds from striking a key as there are fingers. Professor Bonn would urge me to play a note staccato, just one note, "Watch it, see it dance," then say, "Now vary it, watch it, listen. Can you hear the difference?"

This is not a question to excite a grammar school child. Gradually, though, I came to hear something of the keyboard's possible sound effects.

Before the lesson began, he would often have me do this exercise. "Stretch your arms straight ahead at shoulder height toward the keyboard," he would say and survey my arms to see that they were horizontally even, not too high, not too low. "Now drop your hands. Just let them go loose, hanging from the wrist. Feel that weight?" A dutiful nod. "Now keep your hands loose; keep them dropped full weight just as they are, and keeping your arms at the same height, pull your hands part way toward you and bend your elbows out to the side, like this." He would demonstrate, creating the look of a great black-sleeved crow with extended wings bent in half. "Now let the full weight of your forearms and your loose hands just hang there, supported by your shoulders and upper arms. Feel that weight?"[5]

Again I would nod. This tedious old man. When could I play?

"Now let the whole weight go, just drop the whole arm — upper arm, elbow, forearm, hand — into your lap. Plop!"

I obeyed.

Finally we would get to playing.

To this day I sometimes use this exercise to remind myself about weight distribution at the keyboard. Commenting on Rubenstein's mastery of weight control, his use of body and shoulder weight in his forte sections, his relaxed wrists, his ability to elicit a singing tone, Josef Lhévinne sums it up: "There is a vast difference between amateur hammering on the keyboard for force and the more artistic means of drawing the tone from the piano by weight or pressure properly controlled or administered."[6]

Subsequent teachers in high school, twenty years later in Chicago, and now, in Oregon, taught me much. I suspect, however, that the first piano teacher may matter most.

Professor Bonn walked me steadily through scales, arpeggios, chords, and exercises without pushing me through Hanon. Despite his meticulous and rigorous attention to details of technique, somehow what breathed through the lessons was always music, not mechanics. Had it not been so, I surely would have given it up.

I had no desire, ever, to be a professional musician. I was just a determined little girl who wanted to learn how to make music.

MUSICAL FUN

After milling about and chatting over mugs of homemade Northwest Cioppino, accompanied by wine, cheese, bread, and too many sweets, we gather in the long living room near the large twinkling tree. Song sheets appear. I go to the piano. Seated around in chairs and on the floor, guests call out numbers of the songs they want. If the key is too high and they change it on me, I try to fake along, often failing, but nothing stops the singing.

*H*umoroso. Brightly.
Midsummer. The Forties. Madison, Connecticut.

Sun-baked humid days unstitch the straitjacket of ordinary time into a gauzy stretch, elastic as the whims of a twelve- or thirteen-year-old liberated from home for a week, thanks to generous neighbors.

When, near the end of a July day, the flaming disc dips toward the horizon, pinks, yellows, crimsons, blues, and purples streak the distant water-edged heavens. A faint evening breeze lifts. It carries a dense salt smell. Crickets start up their chorus, rowboats are hauled up above the high tide line, children are called home, a pale, hopeful moon appears.

Evening begins to settle in.

Embedded in just such evenings is my strongest early image of how singing and piano playing in a home could generate fun. The scene I create here might occur several times over several summers with slight variations.

If I was lucky in those years between the age of ten and fifteen, my landlocked summer months would be broken by an invitation to join the family across the street for a week or two at the beach. There were four children in the Fitzgerald family: two older girls two years apart, then the boys. I was the oldest by a year, and I understood that part of my function was to mediate tactfully between the two daughters. In the manner of middle-class Connecticut families in the Forties, the mother and children would spend time at a beach cottage, this one rented each summer in Madison, Connecticut. Friday night delivered an influx of fathers from their work in the city — New Haven, Hartford, Waterbury, Bridgeport.

After supper was over, the dishes done, the tracked-in sand swept away, as evening began to fall, children and parents and the occasional weekend guest would sometimes gather in the living room.

The parents mixed their drinks — Scotch, usually, or very dry Martinis. We would get iced tea, lemonade, Coke — something appropriate.

Each of the girls would be asked to play a piece on the dark upright piano that stood over against the stairs leading up to the five bedrooms. All three of us were taking piano lessons from the same teacher in Waterbury: Professor John L. Bonn — a startlingly homely, seemingly ancient pianist and organist who somehow managed, I now realize, to introduce his pupils right away not only to classical piano music but also to a solid dose of music theory.

After each sister had obliged, one of their parents would turn to me. "Will you play something for us?"

I made it a point to be ready. I'd play whatever my remembering fingers held at the time: "Nola," I recall, and later the *Warsaw Concerto*, which I had learned on my own and greatly enjoyed pounding out, and ditto "Malagueña," or more ambitiously, the Chopin Polonaise in A Major. It was many years before a concert in Ottawa by Alicia de la Roccha playing Mozart convinced me for life that the greatest achievement of a pianist is sustained *pianissimo*.

Then Mr. Fitzgerald, an extraordinarily tall man who had to stoop to get through doorways and whose serious face belied his dry wit, would set his drink on top of the piano, bend his long frame over the keyboard, and settle down to play. Anything might come forth, songs from the Thirties, the Forties, show tunes, earlier ballads, melodies somehow familiar even if you didn't know the words.

As he played, my showing-off gland stopped throbbing, the summer twilight outside dimmed to darkness, stars began to appear, the waves continued beating on the beach just outside the front screen door: crash, recede, crash, recede. Mr. Fitzgerald's hands would glide over the keys. Playing. Sometimes we sang, sometimes just listened. He played the way I wanted to, no music before his eyes, fingers finding the keys as if reaching for familiar spots on a lover's body — a thought I certainly would not then have entertained.

I sat there, ice-cold glass in hand, and ached to play like Mr. Fitzgerald.

After a while, if one particular guest had come, the anticipated moment would arrive: "Sing for us, Dan!" Or perhaps Dan, well into his Scotch, rose to his feet unasked, responding to the piano's invitation.

A chubby balding man with bright eyes, round face, and a slight lisp, he stood there in summer slacks and open collar shirt, briefly freed from the intricacies of real estate deals in Waterbury, poised now to entertain us. Drink in one hand, he eyed us all, his demeanor a mix of coyness, droll understatement, and slyness — a voice and manner made for musical comedy.

He moved into the song we waited for:

> Shades of night are creeping
> Willow trees are weeping
> Old folks and babies are sleeping,
> Silver stars are gleaming,
> All alone I'm scheming,
> Scheming to get you out here, my dear —

He sang in almost a whisper, tripping a small dance step in time. Then, as he soft-shoed around the room, drink in hand, his light summer shoes nimbly grazing the freshly swept floorboards, he might pause and lean coyly in toward Mrs. Fitzgerald or one of us as he sang through his lisp:

> Tip-toe to the window, by the window,
> That is where I'll be, come tip-toe
> Thru the tulips with me.
> Tip-toe from your pillow, to the shadow
> Of a willow tree,
> And tip-toe thru the tulips with me.
> Knee deep in flowers we'll stray,
> We'll keep the showers away,

And then, drink carefully balanced, he would drop to one knee before one of us:

> And if I kiss you in the garden
> In the moonlight, Will you pardon me,
> Come tip-toe thru the tulips with me.

Giggles and loud laughs erupted.

Over fifty years later that scene stands clear in memory — the humid July night, the ocean rhythms outside, and the delicious sense of several ambiguities caught, balanced, and released through performance. Fun, that's just what it was. Performance, for sure, but grounded in a keen sense of fun. For me, the musical moment held not only the sense of inclusion as a valued guest, but also a fascinating edge: we were both observers and participants in adult pleasure.

And Mr. Fitzgerald, that tall, distinguished, somewhat remote man, who had a library in his home where he retreated to study and prepare his cases as State's Attorney, that learned man whom we all held in a certain awe, he had at his fingertips, literally, the means of offering us a quiet, seemingly effortless, delight. He appeared to know every Harry Warren / Al Dubin number; Irving Berlin, Cole Porter, Richard Rodgers: these were his fingertips' friends. He played a "Tea for Two" I so envied that I spent hours back home working out my own version by ear.

I knew it required skill and practice to carry off such playing, to say nothing of talent. Still, those evenings at the beach revealed something ultimately more important to me: one could engage in serious academic pursuits, read voraciously, nurse scholarly ambitions, even secretly hope to become a saint (as I then devoutly wished), and still create evenings of fun. One could love Mozart and Beethoven, yet hone another skill at the piano for helping people relax, creating shared pleasure.

Back in our own living room in Waterbury, in a house kept quiet not for a studying father but for a dying one, analogous moments might occur. Pervasive as that quiet was, it did not interfere with my piano playing or practice. And my brother, two years older, found lots of time to play his drums, which sat at the far end of the living room, near the Chickering. Occasionally, when he could tolerate me, we would make music together, I at the piano a stand-in for his records of Mugsy Spanier, Benny Goodman, Harry James, Spike Jones; he staring into early adolescent fog as he morphed via brushes, sticks, and cymbals into young Gene Krupa.

Such interludes—a far cry from Mozart or Haydn waiting in their demure yellow jackets on my G. Schirmer pile—deeply satisfied me. Unlike many of my classmates, I did not take lessons in popular music. I saw, though, from the sheet music I bought with my weekly allowance, that it was easy to read. I could sometimes work out a song on my own, thanks to Professor Bonn, whose musical interests lay leagues distant from "Let's Do It" or "Take Me Out to the Ball Game." I wanted to be able to accompany anyone if the moment arose, as it often would in future years, so I practiced sight-reading and tried to apply, on my own, the basic I–IV–V patterns I'd had to write out and get into my fingers in every key and every position during my first piano years. And although I have not come close to Mr. Fitzgerald's ease at the keyboard, when I decode a song in a fake book today, I owe thanks to Professor Bonn for subjecting me to his unique form of child labor.

Often, as well, a group of my parents' friends would gather on a Saturday night for drinks and socializing. These lifelong friends dwelt in the world of mid-century Roman Catholicism, an understood universe of rooted values and customs. They shared, as well, a vital interest in politics and the stock market. I suppose they talked about Roosevelt, Truman, investing, war and post-war issues. What did I care whether FDR should have another term? Their laughter and voices would float up the stairs to my room where I lay on my bed, ear glued to the Saturday night Hit Parade as I throbbed to the voice of Frank Sinatra.

Then my moment might come. Mr. Kenney, father of my closest childhood friend, was a sweet man with a beautiful tenor voice who many years before had been invited to audition for the Metropolitan Opera.

"Sing us a song, Frank."

I could hear my mother's footsteps coming up the stairs. I was needed to accompany. How the invitation did puff me up—I was needed by adults! With lovable simplicity, Mr.

Kenney would stand by the piano and sing, usually a familiar ballad, like "Danny Boy." Such moments generated a particular kind of pleasure, a musical living-room pleasure that, coupled with their Scotch, certainly made that world of the war and its aftermath a bit warmer. Being able to accompany Mr. Kenney thrilled me.

Fast forward to the early twenty-first century, late Advent, a drizzly evening in Salem, Oregon. In the large house at the end of the street, set in among evergreens blinking with red, green, and silver lights, some thirty or forty folks of various ages have gathered for the annual party. Most have been connected to Willamette University for years, as has our host. Some, new to the faculty, bring small children. Others, newly retired, bring themselves and anecdotes about elderly parents or grandchildren. Many bring just themselves. The deadline for getting exam results to the registrar's office is tomorrow or the next day. Nonetheless, this evening's space is reserved; it holds the desire to gather and to sing.

After milling about and chatting over mugs of homemade Northwest Cioppino, accompanied by wine, cheese, bread, and too many sweets, we gather in the long living room near the large twinkling tree. Song sheets appear. I go to the piano. Seated around in chairs and on the floor, guests call out numbers of the songs they want. If the key is too high and they change it on me, I try to fake along, often failing, but nothing stops the singing.

I love this version of surround sound: the spontaneous hamming up of "The Twelve Days of Christmas" and "The Little Drummer Boy," the variations on "Rudolph the Red-Nosed Reindeer," the quieter rendering of beloved Christmas hymns, "Silent Night" always saved till last. Sometimes Charlie brings out his penny whistle or recorder. Sometimes Jo plays her flute. Now and then we also have Delana's harp.

This is no utopia. We'll all return very shortly to the contradictions, ironies, puzzles, and pain that mark adult life. For the long moment of this evening, however, usefulness, duty, and deadlines are held at bay while voices merge in song.

For all its difference, this is not that far a cry from evenings in Madison or Waterbury, or other evenings in Canada too many to itemize. The pleasure of accompanying voices runs deep and has, in the end, far less to do with performing than with providing a reliable base on which shared pleasure may comfortably rest.

Playing saw me through a high school thin on academic rigor but dense with opportunities to accompany smaller and larger singing groups in recitals, concerts, or on the radio. Through thirteen convent years of near total fast from the piano, assignments to accompany nuns on the organ or teach high school girls' chorus helped keep me in touch with the keyboard.

Unexpected chances to play for and with others still brighten my days. On a recent Fourth of July, two neighbors, both fine singers, baritone and soprano, stopped in with their visiting parents and dog just to sing show tunes for a while, to celebrate the occasion.

Such a moment links across the span of years back to Professor Bonn saying, "For next week, please write out the dominant seventh chord in the key of C in all its positions."

It links back to evenings as a guest at the beach where I learned, close-up, how playing could recreate a room.

It still creates an interval of fun time in a world that needs cheering up, and it carries us out of ourselves to some other welcoming place that we ourselves create and yet find already tastefully furnished by an invisible composer who sensed that our world needed such avenues to musical fun. In such an interval something new always emerges.

COMPOSING FOR CLAIRE

Learning precisely how and where to make those marks on the G or bass clef is work. Tedious. One must be precise. I am not naturally precise. My little notation book has grown tattered through the Claire project, and her music sheets are far from perfect. As I went to work and messed up sheet after sheet each year, I drew odd comfort from knowing that Schubert left a big ink blot on the manuscript of his "Trout Quintet."

It's a simple story. A new being enters the world. I feel the urge to celebrate, search for an appropriate gesture.

Decide that each year I'll compose a piece on the piano to celebrate this birth, this mystery of growth, this unanticipated enlargement of family.

Granddaughter arrives.

Rejoice.

Simple story.

Except that no story is simple.

Foreign elements intrude, enrich, complicate the narrative. Backstory from one's life makes itself felt at unexpected moments. Nonetheless, the basic plot line has continued now through fourteen birthdays. Each November, a piece composed by Grandma Cookie appears, in black ink on colored paper, three holes punched so Claire can insert it into her special binder, *Claire's Musikbüchlein*.

As I write this, I've come to the end of the project. That "baby" is now a happy, talented fourteen-year-old who already knows her nimble way around the keyboard, can improvise her own songs and make her full-sized cello sing. After I played Claire her birthday piece last year, I turned to her and said, "This is it, Claire. You're going off to a new adventure in a few months. High school. No more annual birthday pieces; you will be into a new life. If you fall in love, though, call me up, and I'll see if I can compose you a ballad."

From the end, now, I survey the fourteen years and wonder just why I did it.

What sustained me through this work? And what do they really add up to, these notated pieces celebrating a child's growth into young womanhood?

As Chebutykin, the weary doctor in Chekhov's *Three Sisters* so effectively intones in the face of futile human effort, "What difference does it make?"

Time's passing intensifies this question for me.

I was not naive. I had a pretty good sense of the effort it would require. Nor did I feel particularly confident. On the contrary, I felt embarrassed, and at the same time a bit pretentious, when I finally said to my son and daughter-in-law, "Every year I hope to write a piece for Claire's birthday." They took it calmly.

I had never thought I'd become a grandmother. Religious life cancels any such expectation. So now the surprised Grandma Cookie would try to compose.

In the early years I played *for* her. In recent years I've played with her, improvised to her bass, read a four-hand composition with her, or jointly fooled around on the keyboard.

Sometimes musical aptitude develops slowly. Other times a leap occurs. A few years ago, after her tenth birthday, I jotted down an anecdote to catch my sense of such a leap. My husband and I were winding up an overnight visit to Seattle. To while away a few moments on this slow Saturday morning, Claire was, at her dad's request, playing for us Beethoven's Sonatina in G, the first movement. When she finished, I asked her, "Want to have some fun and out-Beethoven Beethoven?"

Always game, she slid over on the piano bench, and I sat down at the top end. We were familiar with this arrangement from playing duets. As she again played Beethoven, I fumbled some harmonies in the upper register in the key of G. She was wedded to notes, of course, yet saw me wandering around the keyboard without sheet music in front of me as I searched for what was possible in the moment.

She knew I'd been studying jazz improvisation for a few years, and after years of reading classical and pop music, I was trying to free myself from depending on notation.

"Play the scale of G for me," I asked.

Easily done. Nimble little fingers.

"Now show me the triad of G major."

Easily done.

"D major, then C major."

Ditto.

Ready to roll.

"As I play, just watch my left hand," I said. I showed her again the three basic triads she had just moments before so easily located.

"Now, I'll play the top that Beethoven wrote for us, but you keep your eye on my left hand and you'll see he's using exactly the chords you just played for me."

We fooled around with this a bit. The whole process occupied perhaps five minutes. It was fun. And then she was off to play with Delilah, the cat.

Once again, I felt grateful to my first piano teacher, Professor John L. Bonn, who assigned me, long before Claire's age, to write out chords and symbols for the tonic (I), subdominant (IV), and dominant (V) in a specified key before each lesson. It seemed so useless then, a total bother unrelated to this exciting new power of calling forth music from a keyboard. I was, however, an earnest child.

Now, I was traveling back into that simple exercise routine, which cramped my writing fingers each week before I got ready to walk to my music lesson after school, be propped up on the requisite number of yellow G. Schirmer albums before the black Steinway of Professor Bonn in his large clapboard home on Willow Street Extension in Waterbury, Connecticut. My weekly lesson from age seven to thirteen cost three dollars.

As I began, what immediately mattered to me was finding something less transient than rubber duckies, Dr. Seuss, Legos, Mary Poppins, Harry Potter, or Kit the American Girl. What could I offer that might hold some meaning for a new child in this new world when she turned sixteen, say, or twenty? Make that fifty. In any case, searching for a more lasting gesture, I chose the most evanescent of gifts: music. There is no holding onto its sounds, no catching it, possessing it as a thing. You cannot stand and study it as you might a painting. As its sounds come to life, they fade. Nonetheless, I thought, I would use each piece to chart her years and celebrate the milestone called "birthday."

One small moment solidified my resolve.

Shortly after Claire was born, my husband and I went out for dinner at McGrath's, a local fish restaurant. As usual, we chatted with our waitress, this time a slim, shy student at the university from which I'd just retired. Suddenly, in the course of our exchange, she said "My grandpa writes songs for me," and her face lit up.

Her words touched me. Her delight. And I remembered that. Her grandpa had bridged time and found a way into her heart. He had, moreover, offered her access to a bit of joy. Could I do that?

Timing mattered, too. Claire had chosen the perfect

moment to appear in my life. Composing for her fit right into my hopes and goals for retirement: to make music in many different forms and ways. Besides, I sometimes like a challenge.

In one sense, the first three years were the easiest. Year one: "Claire's First Piece," on bright pink paper. Year two: "Claire's Tango," on bright green. Year three: "Claire's Waltz," on gray. I wanted a different bright color for each year. Heavier stock paper, I hoped, might withstand the turning of pages by grimy fingers in years to come.

For the first attempt, on its bright pink stock, I aimed for melody, a singing quality. In the key of E-flat, it is meticulously written out, replete with signals for dynamics, phrasing, and tempo. Where do musical ideas come from? I cannot answer that clearly. If I play a few tones on the piano, sometimes one tone seems to call for another, or a group of tones to carry it forward. Perhaps it's a bit like people who hum as they work, not humming "a piece" really, but somehow pulling sounds out of mind and ear and air to go pleasingly together. I wanted something singable. For a while, I kept a messy notebook about this process, and tucked into that, I now find this note: *The fascination for me of what leads to what, what goes to what?* You fool around with tones, see where they may take you. For me, that occurs at the keyboard. As I worked each year, questions would arise that echoed similar perplexities I'd had in writing fiction. How do you get a sense of direction? How do you make an ending? What can repetition achieve? You try one thing, then another. In fiction-making or music-making, you are not so much following a path as making up the path you follow, even as you travel. Surprise is a key element, for composer as well as for reader or listener.

In his little book, *Design in Music*, Gerald Abraham makes this seemingly simple observation: once a composer has conceived the first musical idea or motive, the basic problem is how to go on.[7] She faces a choice: repeat that thought, exactly or altered, or say something different. How many times over the years had I faced that basic problem with a half-written page of text in front of me. Now it was a keyboard.

I started work on the first piece in January, two months after her birth, aiming to complete it for her first birthday the following November. Delivering it on time didn't matter while she was a baby, but I would try. In addition to revising a long novel during those months, at the keyboard, I was swinging between learning Brahms's waltzes for piano four hands and Dvořák's *Slavonic Dances* with my piano partner, memorizing a Beethoven bagatelle, and deciphering harmonic progressions in a bit of the "Waldstein Sonata." Playing the "Waldstein" is far beyond my powers, but this particular passage drew me deeply. I hoped I might in some way be able to use what it taught me, for Claire. I've never formally studied theory, never had a course in music history, so figuring out connections between chords, where they go, how they might combine, has been learned a little here, a little there, over the years.

I sounded out the passage over and over. Then, I plotted out the right hand and saw that it was built on five notes of the E-major scale, starting on G sharp and working down to C sharp and then back up to G sharp before finally dipping again to stop on F sharp. Beethoven is taking us on a simple little trip via *mi re do ti la ti do*, much like the soprano's vocal exercises we endured morning after morning from open windows next door on South Hyde Park Boulevard in Chicago. Context is all. It's what Beethoven puts with this little nursery rhyme melody, how he voices the chords that support it., transforming a simple few tones into an excursion fathoms deep. So straightforward, yet so haunting. My numbers here, charting his course, look sterile and dull: I-V-vi-III7-IV-V-I-ii-I-V-I. Near the expected end of this phrase, he dips down to leave us hanging on a dominant B-seventh, that tone that "cries to go home." And finally, as if to say, "Don't miss this," he immediately repeats the whole pattern an octave below. It's a truly beautiful tease, a short adventure taking us away from a secure home (in the key of E) through ridges of change in nearby neighborhoods, toward a momentary alighting in a secondary home (key of A). Then he turns us around with soul stirring chords to lead us back to true security, our home. My words limp in expressing the profundity of this brief trip, one he'll repeat in various ways in pages that follow. For years, this passage had haunted me. I wanted somehow to use it.

To do that, I'd have to transpose it to the key I was working in for Claire. I did this, and thereby came to know in a deeper way the power of the single tone (the lovely E natural in the F-minor chord), but here's the important thing: *I never did use it*. There was no place for it.

Hours of work down the drain. Still, there's no way to know if that's true, for perhaps new musical synapses were created in my brain. My Beethoven excursion joined, so to speak, bulging files of cast-offs from fictional efforts: plots, dialogue bits, fabulous unused ideas. Learning to discard matters. I knew about Beethoven's notebooks, Gershwin's tune book. Our universe resounds with musical possibilities, tones unsounded, chords unheard.

Maybe Keats had it right: Unheard melodies are sweeter.

Early on I learned, as well, the value of stealing, of heeding echoes in the head. In year two, when I wanted to compose a tango, Bizet clarified the rhythm for me. (Ten years later, the baby-become-star would herself play the "Habenera" from *Carmen* in her own piano recital.)

When, for her third birthday, I wanted to produce a waltz, I turned for inspiration to a favorite: Scott Joplin's "Bethena." The singing melody, the regular waltz time, the dance-ableness of it all — I wanted to achieve something like that.

Gretchen and I were at that time playing Brahms's Sixteen Waltzes, op. 39. Though Brahms is nowhere on my notated page, who knows what ultimately etches our lines in time?

Next came a significant roadblock: Interruption. I knew well that major interruption could kill a writer's infant idea. A big trip, a family crisis — how do you sustain momentum in your project? In fiction writing, especially in the early, tentative stages of a story, my own limit for sustaining the zip of story-in-process was about three days. After that, significant loss. I would resort to writing telegraphic notes to myself on bits of paper. Nevertheless, days passed, golden bits turned to dross, recycling bins overflowed.

In February, my husband and I went to Hawaii for a week. Maui, long on oceanfront and open time, offered no piano. I feared losing the thread of Claire's piece. One morning, lying alone on the beach, I tried humming out tunes on the *do re mi* scale. Years of using a pitch pipe to teach nuns Gregorian chant paid off. I hummed the thread of Claire's piece on *do re mi* up to the point where it could go one of several ways. It seemed to work. I could hold these bits in my head. Reassured, I sank into the sand.

Two or three weeks after we came home, I was able to return to the piece at last. Thanks to solfège, it had remained with me. Better yet, I discovered that as I walked around the neighborhood or to the library, I could hum parts of it, even imagine other musical possibilities, away from the keyboard. This was new and encouraging. As a rule, I don't walk around with tunes in my head.

Each year after that, early October signaled time to begin Claire's work. In late November, I'd deliver the piece to her mom and dad as she crawled and ran about, blissfully unaware. I'd play it for them. Then, her copy would be slipped into the special notebook. In her third year, she noticed and asked what that was all about. Her mom explained "Each year, Grandma Cookie is writing a piece for your birthday." "Okay," she grinned, and watched it go into the book and then into the closet alongside rain gear, scarves, boots.

When Claire turned four, she was in play-school. She had little friends.

She was beginning to name her own expanding world. That year I smartened up.

Words, that's what we need, words to articulate her sense of her world. And so now each piece would try to say something about her evolving life, and the task grew both simpler and more complicated. Simpler, because I cast off earlier ambitions. In the beginning, facing a blank musical slate, I'd been thinking in terms of musical genres: a minuet, say, a waltz, a rhapsody, and so on. Now, I could think about Claire — her life, its pieces — and how to get some of that musically onto a page so we could sing it.

Claire, four years old, highly verbal, was already diddling on the piano. One quick look at the lyrics of her Fourth Birthday Song tells the tale:

> My name is Claire Eliz-a-beth Furt-wangler,
> My daddy's name is Thomas Ga-vin,
> My mommy's name is Ly-anda Lynn Haupt,
> We all live here in West Seattle.
> Chick-wicki, yell-ow mell-ow, live with us.
> Cuck-y, luck-y, Clem-en-tine,
> They sure can make a fuss.
> But sometimes when we sneak a peek,
> To see what's in their nest
> We find a big sur-prise,
> And the green ones are the best!

The song went on to describe her weekly schedule — swimming, playing, school, her closest friends — and ended with a look toward the next year. Minuets and rhapsodies had bit the dust; I had landed on musical earth.

We sang it together with Claire, and then she danced to it. Next day, when we were in the car, Claire, along with her mom and dad, began to belt out, "My name is Claire Elizabeth Furtwangler." I felt I'd hit a bull's eye.

Then came five, pre-school, and the years thereafter — real school.

What would a five-year-old only child want to hear about her life? There were her friends — Vanja, Kashia, Amy,

Peter — her teachers, her swimming lessons, her ballet lessons, her Sunday School teachers. There were as well her chickens and Anni, the hostile cat. Oh yes, the gerbil. Forget the gerbil. Focus on the star herself.

So I scrunched my knees under her child's-size yellow table, took a sheet of her orange paper and a crayon, and quizzed her. When I could pry her attention away from the little girl's mirror over her table, she answered my questions. I wrote it all down, went home, and got to work.

Over the years, Claire's interviews expanded. At eleven, she filled out a long email questionnaire about the personalities of her latest chickens, her current best friends, her favorite authors and singers. Later, she included what she hoped to be and do with her life. Basically this boiled down to saving the world, starting with the environment. More recent answers, at thirteen and fourteen, added the note, "I'll write and sing music, and become a star."

Someone once asked George Gershwin which came first, music or words. He had no patience with the question. I sympathize. I cannot describe the process exactly, but I know instinctively that some phrases, some lines, are more singable than others. I fool around at the keyboard, I look at the interview notes, make up a little ditty that might rhyme a bit, try it out. Claire's life grows full; my words sound dull. I am no Ira Gershwin or Cole Porter. How to feed into a little song the exotic experiences of being kissed by an African giraffe in Kenya, practicing cello, walking with Masai warriors, liking Cat Stevens, listening to mom on her violin, dad on his African drums? How to make a whole out of such disparate scraps? Bits of paper are strewn on the floor around my piano bench. Bach composed his Mass in B Minor by assembling pieces. Too early to know what's a discard.

Chance favors the prepared mind.

Dull days can feel oh so very dull. As I scratched away on Claire's latest, a sheet flew off the music stand, and there, revealed, stood music from *The Magic Flute*. Mozart — it's hard to imagine him dull — leapt to my rescue, handing me "Papageno's Song." Into Claire's piece went a bit of Mozart. Not to be outdone, Beethoven made his contribution to the same composition, a phrase from the engaging "Alla danza tedesca" from the String Quartet in B-flat Major, op. 130. Three years later, Jerome Kern saved me with a line from "Smoke Gets in Your Eyes" to hold a list of Claire's current friends.

Around the time of her tenth birthday, Claire went onstage to sing, but not where you might expect. With enviable composure, she climbed the steps to the far end of the sanctuary at Holy Rosary Church, turned to face a packed congregation, and sang into the microphone the beautiful Alleluia for the First Sunday of Advent. A few days later came her birthday song:

> Here's my song for birthday ten,
> Full of me and my life again,
> Some things new and some things old,
> Listen up and you will be told.

This intro held a surprise: it was sung to the melody of her "Alleluia."

I wanted to honor a child's growing life, make a little singable record of her childhood. From the beginning, I recognized it as a feint against time's sickle. Then, too, I'd lived long enough in music's forever fading frame to know that for any song to last past the birthday itself, I'd have to notate it. How else have composers, for centuries, tried to nail down what's constantly disappearing? On the other hand, how persistently, too, have musicians resisted being tied to the notes, followed their impulse to move off the sheet, so to speak, and sing their own songs? I would notate Claire's pieces as well as I could, but try to leave her some room.

Learning precisely how and where to make those marks on the G or bass clef is work. Tedious. One must be precise. I am not naturally precise. My little notation book has grown tattered through the Claire project, and her music sheets are far from perfect. As I went to work and messed up sheet after sheet each year, I drew odd comfort from knowing that Schubert left a big ink blot on the manuscript of his "Trout Quintet." I was fascinated to learn about a Beethoven manuscript newly discovered in 2005. This eighty-four-page, four-hand piano version of his *Grosse Fuge* showed Beethoven's intense physicality as he wrote: holes gouged by erasures, splattered ink, measures canceled out with crosshatches, smudges from wiped-away wet ink, high notes soaring far above the staff. Who knows what agitation, urgency, frustration this evidence suggests as Beethoven — old, sick, stone deaf — pressed symbols into the paper just eight months before he died? One more teasing example: a recent display of a Chopin manuscript at the Morgan Library included a satiric sketch of Mozart doodled onto the page by Chopin as he was notating. I've had good company in finding this task a drag. White-out became my new best friend.

More recent birthday pieces have grown thinner on notation, particularly the bass notes. Melodies remain intact, but directions for phrasing and dynamics have almost disappeared. Claire is developing her own sense of both. Above each bar, I've simply indicated the appropriate chord: C7, F minor, and so on. Sometimes I was lazy or short on time that November. Other factors have been at work, too. During the years since Claire's sixth birthday, I've been slowly moving through my own musical evolution, learning to read jazz lead sheets more quickly, trying to decipher more accurately the chord symbols above the melodies in my jazz Real Book. Lessons in improvisation have terrified me, but also loosened me up. I've come to see more possibilities at the keyboard, developed more courage to try them out.

As I put down those black symbols on Claire's pages, I want them to be an avenue to discovery, not a box to fit into. The words are fixed, of course, but for the music in later pieces, I've simply put down clues to the harmonic structure. Maybe someday Claire will look at them and a light will go on: Ah, I could play it this way . . . or that way . . . or another way. She might move through the portal of those symbols toward richer musical avenues. If it never happens, that's fine; the song remains there, words and music recording her moments in time.

At the end of her ninth birthday song, I added this to her tune in 4/4 time, key of C major: *To finish, play anything you want, using C G F chords in any order, as long as you end with a C chord and keep the basic rhythm of the piece. Bravo!*

As I told Claire with her fourteenth birthday piece, "This is it." I felt relieved, glad I'd persevered, and ready to call it done. Still, I wanted to wrap it up, make the ending more tangible. I decided I'd find a way to get a CD made of all the songs. I knew, even then, that by the time she might want to hear them again, CDs would be long gone. You do what you can do, and that was what I could do.

Once again, I was lucky. After asking around — friends, musicians, singers — I found my singer. My aging voice sometimes cracks; Jill's voice is lovely and, besides, she had a real feeling for her own grandmother and was instinctively enthusiastic about the project. So she undertook a substantial task: learning melodies and lyrics to ten new songs, some outside her normal singing range. An experienced improviser and sound engineer said he would do the recording. And so arrived a unique moment: I sat at the great Steinway on the university's Hudson Hall Music Center stage and played Claire's songs while Jill sang and Mike recorded us. A few days later came the editing session. Shortly thereafter, the CD was made.

And again, as if the gods favored this task, I found a talented graphic designer to make the CD cover and design the inserted booklet to carry all the words, and a few small shots of the star herself at various stages.

Christmas came. The CD was delivered.

As I look back now, some aspects of this venture seem clear, but the desire to do it caught me by surprise. I did wish to celebrate this unexpected turn in my life and honor a new being's arrival in this strange and baffling world. To mark it annually by making songs simply felt, well, right. Then too, I'd seen the light in that waitress' eyes. I sensed that however modest the project's outcome, that would be fine. It would require work, but also maybe offer a bit of fun. As for the basic itch to compose songs, I'd felt that before in other circumstances, but never to celebrate such a joyful event.

Music subverts the inevitability of ending. Decades ago, those shakily penciled-in symbols on my childhood's music pages had opened portals to another world my aged teacher could never have imagined. They had led to years of discovery and pleasure. More recently, another teacher had opened even more doors into musical freedom through improvisation.

Who can fathom how layers of our years work their way into the songs we sing of our own lives, or the stories we tell of others? A written symbol lies flat on the page, as do these words on this page. Yet as any reader knows, a symbol implies acres of meaning. Exploring that space has occupied musicians and readers for centuries. My words and the notes written on those brightly colored pages are not bound just to the pages. They constitute a symbolic gesture as much toward the future as toward the present birthday. They spring from a mix of realism and hope, heartfelt gratitude set forth in odd looking black symbols sprinkled across messy pages to sing a life.

And so, not surprisingly, the story of composing for Claire turns out to be not so simple.

HUNGER

Here I sit, replenished by Schubert who, dead at thirty-one, could never know of his gift to me, a tourist with tired feet in a Dublin art gallery, May, 2000.

Dublin, May 27, 2000. I am sitting in the upper-level gallery of the National Gallery of Art. My feet hurt.

In front of me, Jesus feeds the multitudes from a basket of bread, courtesy of Giovanni Lanfranco. It's a very large painting. Those crowded around Jesus — babies, mothers, weary-looking men talking and gesticulating — also seem eager and hungry. Very hungry. Probably their feet hurt too.

To my right, a larger than life stone sculpture by Ferdinand Dietz depicts Cronos eating one of his children. He holds the child at a twisted angle, head down, exposed face contorted in pain. Feet and ankles are already gone, and part of his arms.

This moment's motif: appetite.

On the left, two paintings away, hangs another Lanfranco painting: Jesus at the Last Supper, blessing a round loaf of bread, whole wheat perhaps.

And in between these two paintings I see a depiction of muscular men in *Peter Finding the Tribute Money*, by Peter

Paul Rubens; coins are scattered on the ground, and in the lower left corner is a single skull.

My appetite for visual art is limited. Art museums quickly tire me.

A different hunger keeps me rooted here. To my right, a staircase winds down to the Shaw Room where, two days ago, we lucked upon singers, the National Chamber Chorus, presenting a selection of opera arias and show tunes that included a particularly touching duet rendition of "Only Make Believe."

Yet now, at this moment, something beyond make-believe floats up to me, up up the staircase and around this room of greedy mortals trapped forever in their hunger: the cascading crystalline sounds of the "Trout Quintet." John O'Connor is at the piano.

The runs and intricate melodic conversation of the "Trout Quintet" feed me. There's this feeling that I ought to be looking. I'm in an art gallery, for heaven's sake. But I want to sit and hear and listen. And Schubert, bless him, meets my soul's need. In these moments, the sparkling "Trout" transcends my sense of horror and pain in Irish history memorialized in historical sites I've so recently visited: the scarred General Post Office; the flinty fascination of the Burren and Poulnabrone; the brooding power of silent ancient megaliths; all the traces of a peat-buried civilization that grew hungry, ate, drank, hammered elegant bronze, made monks, music, and Anna Livia Plurabelle. It's all somehow caught and dispersed in this moment, thanks to Schubert. The sounds float by and around and through me. And surely even the lonely skull in that painting might once have been so fed. I hope he heard such music.

Grafton Street awaits — immersion in the raging Celtic Tiger. But here, for now, it is melody that sings throughout the silent walls of art. O'Connor has begun the variations, those playful melodious turnings this way and that.

I have left the ancient burial mounds, the visions of art, the vendors of Grafton Street, and here I sit, replenished by Schubert, who could never know of his gift to me, a tourist with tired feet in a Dublin art gallery, May, 2000. For lunch I shall order trout.

WHY ORNAMENTS HERE?

Little ornaments come sprinkling through our days, embellishing the moment, the hour.

"**D**ress it up! Add a bit of flair." Stick a sprig of parsley on the fish, add a bright scarf on the dark dress, multiply the Christmas lights. The desire to embellish, to dress up drab reality is universal.

Ornamentation in notated piano music can be brief — a trill, a turn — or extended. It can slow down the sight-reader. What is this thing? A mordent, a trill, a turn, appoggiatura? And how do my fingers execute it? By no means random, ornaments are related in some way — obvious or hidden — to the melody or harmony of the moment.[8]

Little ornaments come sprinkling through our days, embellishing the moment, the hour. Fleeting or repeated, quickly forgotten, they can spread like an arpeggio over larger chunks of life in a kind of echo chain, picking up harmony or dissonance and turning it, however briefly, into something else — a surprise, a lift. Such ornaments can alter us, though we may recognize it only later, stuck in memory.

So I sprinkle these bits through longer essays here because

they have mattered in the composing of the life I notate. How do we finally know what is crucial to the song of life? It may be as tiny as a sharp or flat, as limited as a phrase, as telling as a hint of modulation into a different key.

IMPROVISING

Whatever the inner dimensions of the improvising experience, it's clear to me that at a certain level improvising means giving up (or going beyond) the superficial level of control we amateurs have struggled so hard to acquire.

LEARNING TO RELISH RISK

In *The Time of Our Singing*, Richard Powers's elegant novel about music, family, race, and twentieth-century America, he creates an episode in which the narrator, Joseph, a gifted classical pianist studying at Juilliard, happens upon the universe of keyboard improvisation. One afternoon, he interrupts his friend Wilson Hart in the practice room where Will should be exercising his voice but instead spends hours at the piano, composing. Will slides over on the piano bench. "Sit down. We're going to make something happen." He has been playing part of the second movement of the Rodrigo guitar concerto. First the two of them play "straight," and then suddenly Will breaks free.

"Before I knew what was happening, his fingers dropped into bottomless places. They untied the long, mournful melody and lifted out the contents hidden inside."

103

Joseph tries to limp after Will on the keyboard, but feels his fingers as "clubs."

"I knew the shape of the music he made. You couldn't live in this country and not breathe it. But I'd never learned the rules, the laws of freedom that kept those improvisations aloft, just out of reach of a clean conservatory death."[9]

Surprised by Joseph's inability to keep up with him, Will asks afterward, "You can't make it go, on its own? You need it out there, in front of you, on the page?" He offers friendly cold comfort, "Don't make no difference, brother Joe. Some folks need the notes. Other folks don't even care what the notes are called."

I need the notes. Yet I long to be able to improvise, to learn how to make music "go on its own." Like Will, I have at various times glimpsed another way to relate to the keyboard, a way that uncovers music hidden within music, unties it, sets it free.

Such moments have left me wondering and curious. What is composition? What is performance? How do they relate? What is music, anyhow? Where is it, where does it come from, and where does it go? When Horowitz says the music is underneath the notes, what does he mean? When Neuhaus advises the student to play away from the notes, what does he mean? What is the relation of notation to music? How many different ways are there to make music?[10]

I cannot answer these questions. I can, however, honor the spirit of creative play that releases music from written or simply heard music or, as Joseph puts it, launches "possibility out of empty air." In his classic study of the play element in culture, Johann Huisinga cites "earnest" as the opposite of "play." I am earnest about desiring to learn this kind of play.[11]

For me to write about improvisation seems almost presumptuous, for I am a beginner. The keyboard my fingers have roamed over since I was seven sometimes feels like a stranger whose possibilities I haven't yet fathomed. I've stood by pianists and marveled at how freely they play without the page, without those enticing black shapes asking the player to release music from, beneath, within, beyond, around them.

Along the way, I've learned how to read a lead sheet printed only with notes of the melody and the chord symbols. I can fill in the left hand with most conventional chords, and my hands can travel some kinds of distance over the keyboard reasonably well. Still, to feel secure I need to read the notes.

Joseph spends days and weeks training his ear, brain, and hands to reconnect with the keyboard in a new way. Finally, he returns to the piano with Will, and they successfully improvise. Will sets the theme. They send out challenges, dares, teases to each other, carrying on a musical conversation.

Reflecting on the experience, Joseph comments, "Everything we'd done — the free-form quotes, the random wandering — was just a huge unlimbering of the harmonic journey hidden in the original material." How does one addicted to reading music learn to make such a journey?

Twenty years ago, I found myself in Princeton, New Jersey, where my husband was a member of the Institute for Advanced Study for a year.

Back home, in eastern Canada, I had been studying organ for a couple of years and trying to practice on the university chapel organ for an hour or two each weekday morning while the children were in school. Once a week, I also played four-hand piano with my partner, Albert Spatz, and practiced for that as often as I could. On Saturday mornings, he and I spent our first two hours or so playing our current project, then spent the last hour sight-reading. Sometimes, at home, my husband and I doodled through songs of the 1920s and '30s on banjo and piano. Finally, on Sundays, I often accompanied the choir at Mass in our little mission church on its small, inadequate electric organ.

Now, here we were. No children to tend (our sons were away at school), no Sunday Mass duties, no classes to meet, no papers to grade. I had a big writing project to deal with: revising a long novel in which a major publisher had shown interest. I could give several hours a day to that, with time left over. Before many months passed, I arranged to take organ lessons and practice on the magnificent instrument in the Princeton University chapel. I also answered an ad for "organist needed" and played on a few Sundays in a small Protestant church in a neighboring town.

Still, I felt the itch to launch out into new musical territory. I wanted at long last to learn something about improvisation. After one academic year, we would return to our small town in the Maritimes. It would be back to organ, four-hand piano, Mass, motherhood, and the rest of it. This was my chance.

Westminster Choir School was offering an evening course in jazz improvisation once a week. Summoning nerve, I called the teacher, Laurie Altman. I would be in Princeton for only one year, I explained, but I wanted to learn what I could.

"What can you do?" he asked.

My heart sank. Though I had been classically trained as a child, my playing in subsequent decades had been sporadic, all over the lot.

"I can find my way around triads in the I-IV-V positions in most keys," I said.

"I can read an easy lead sheet. That's about it." I was not naive about the work involved.

"We'll go far beyond that," he said briskly. I couldn't read his tone: threat, challenge, invitation, warning? How would I practice? We had no piano in the apartment.

In the small community center at the Institute, I discovered an old upright with a couple of lazy keys. Then after a few months, strangers offered me a rare gift. Through a mutual friend, neighbors who lived just outside the Institute grounds heard of my desire for a better piano. They gave me a key to their house, which was empty during the day while they were at work. Thereafter, when possible, I walked a couple of blocks, took my place at their magnificent Steinway, and worked on

Laurie's assignment for the week. I tried to spend a couple of hours there each afternoon. But it was never enough.

At the Choir School, we met weekly in a small classroom: five students, Laurie, and a grand piano. I was the rank beginner. Three of the others, two men of early middle age and a woman in her mid-thirties, had played or were playing in clubs and places around Princeton. One had played for years in the Marine Band and now played downtown, off Nassau Street, in a popular Princeton spot. The oldest in the class, whom Laurie called his wunderkind, had taken up jazz playing after he retired and could now play a mean stride piano. Marshal had started late and persevered. He gave me heart.

Laurie, all business, good-humored and focused, pushed us to work hard. He made you want to work, a great teacher's gift. He had the talent of breaking down a process, showing us parts and connections, eliciting from each of us what we could do, encouraging us toward progressively more difficult assignments. To write about that experience, I've resurrected my carefully stored notebooks. When I look at these notes now — the scales, drills, harmonic progressions, modulation patterns, voicings, arrangements I worked out during that year, plus pages of information and exercises in reserve for future reference — I'm astonished at how much we covered in those ten months and dismayed at the heaps I have totally forgotten.

Laurie taught us many elements of improv with examples, exercises, running commentary, and humor. He demonstrated the development of rhythmic and melodic motifs, how to pull out harmonic progressions implied in a tune, how to travel away from them and return, how to connect scales and triads. And he expected us to find ways to use this in arrangements he set us to making on our own.

He would illustrate something on the piano, and in that moment, it seemed clear. A day later, I would sit down at the kind strangers' keyboard and go blank. My hands, my hands, why wouldn't they just obey? But what were they to obey? The brain? Why did my brain seem dead? In class I had felt excited to understand what he was doing. Now I could find a chord or two, but where was I supposed to go from there?

Halfway through the course, after composing several so-so arrangements, I worked out an arrangement of "Hackensack" that I liked. The first section was written as a boogie-woogie and then, in section B, I shifted into stride style. It took me considerable time, and I was proud of it.

Then came the dreaded moment in class when I had to leave my chair, go to the piano, and face the keyboard. Alone. No words, no excuses. Alone, alone, all all alone. The keyboard was my sea, my life jacket a written-out eraser-smudged score sitting there before my eyes. Would it hold me above the waves?

I played my boogie and hoped for the best.

Laurie, always encouraging, waited for a few thoughtful moments.

"That shows a lot of work," he offered. "You've made an effective arrangement." Long pause. "But you need to get free of notes."

Exactly.

A year was not long enough to accomplish that. In late summer, we returned to the old life in New Brunswick. Daily demands had to be met. Our son Andrew would be back with us. Tom remained away at school.

The notebooks from Laurie Altman went into cold storage.

Fast forward twenty years.

The children, now no longer children, have vanished into their own lives.

A new keyboard is mine here in Salem, Oregon: a Steinway grand piano I never expected to own. For many years in Canada I had relished weekly duet sessions with my partner on his Steinway L. How I had loved its tone.

In Oregon, I one day said to my friend Anita Sullivan, a poet and piano tuner, "If word of an available Steinway L ever comes your way, let me know."

"Little chance of that," she replied. "Folks want to hold on to an L." Shortly thereafter, her unexpected phone call came. She was looking at an L that had to be sold by its owner. "Interested?" Several hours later, the deal was struck. I had my cherished Steinway L.

I have played the university organ a bit since coming here, but now have put that aside for good. A congenial and talented four-hand partner plays with me each week. My husband and I occasionally play banjo and piano together. Now and then, as time allows, I play with a flutist and a cellist who live nearby. Add to such pleasures considerable time spent playing old classical favorites and reading through new ones. A fair amount of musicking fills my week. In addition, the nearby university offers frequent chances to hear live music, and the Pacific Northwest abounds in such opportunities.

Soon after I retired from teaching, I learned that there is an experienced improviser here in town, a skillful teacher named Julian Snow. The buried spark flickers. Could I make enough progress in, say, five to seven years to feel somewhat comfortable "writing in air?" I am not willing to abandon other kinds of musicking. This will be an add-on, but I mean to stick with it. Can I do it? Then I remember the moment years ago when my feet, seemingly on their own, began to find notes on the organ pedalboard, a facility I had worked on for months. Drill, that's the answer. I believe in drill.

Shoot for the stars . . . and drill to get there.

For over a year, I think about contacting Julian Snow. The demon of doubt grows busy: I don't know enough theory; I never studied it; I never had a course in music history; my fingers need more drill; I've never had ear training; I don't spend time listening to jazz; am I disciplined enough to take this on?

I think of eager students in my fiction-writing classes, brimming with ideas and certain that their first novel, published to rave reviews, lay just the other side of their final grade. Oh, for such naiveté.

Why do I hesitate so long?

Improvisation antedates the gradual emergence of notation. A musician musicked — composed, played, made music — alone or with others. Our modern hard and fast distinctions between composer, performer, and audience took centuries to evolve and owe much, Christopher Small argues, to the development of Western industrial society with its implicit values and class structures.[12] In any case, the custom of public performance, replete with concert hall, soloist on stage, hired orchestra, conductor with score, paying patrons — these elements were not firmly in place in the Western classical tradition until the mid-nineteenth century.

Developing a usable system of written symbols to represent musical sound — pitch and duration — took a millennium, at least. The ancient Greeks had a letter system. Neumes seem to have appeared toward the end of the first century. Subsequent periods trace a complex evolution of sign-for-sound systems up to the one still used today and then onward to the radical experiments of twentieth-century avant-garde composers such as Cage, Stockhausen, and others who have either moved from or highlighted the inadequacies of our familiar system by imagining alternatives. Slonimsky notes Penderecki's directive to play "the highest possible sounds of the instrument" and John Cage's unfathomable directive: "This is a composition indeterminate of its performance, and the performance is of actions which are often indeterminate of themselves."[13]

Although no graphic symbol can adequately represent the pitch and duration of each sound, I suspect that for most of us who learned piano as children, our first great challenge was twofold: to train our hands and to decode notation. We were taught to trust what we read.

Look at the page. Look at your hands. Look at the keyboard. Connect. I watch my six-year-old granddaughter concentrate as she does this. She grows impatient with herself, tosses her hair back in frustration when she reads something inaccurately or her fingers fumble. Straying from the text means making a mistake. Earnest, she wants to get it right.

I know the feeling.

In the notationless musical universe, a musician composed and a musician improvised. Even chanting monks improvised. We know that improvising skills were de rigueur for composers up to 1750 and certainly appeared frequently after that. Monteverdi expected his singers to improvise the line. We thank Bach for eventually turning many of his prodigious improvisings into notated music. Stories about Mozart's improvising abound. Beethoven's legendary improvisations are said to have moved listeners to tears and surpassed his public performances. As for taking a theme and running with it, for this he was notorious, as was Liszt and, in another musical world decades later, the great Art Tatum.[14]

Learning to read notation and learning to improvise went hand in hand, so to speak. What mattered was exploring an instrument's possibilities for making music alone or in play with other instruments, including the human voice.

Bach's older brother Christoph (who was himself taught by Pachelbel) taught young Johann Sebastian. Christoph Wolff, in his *Johann Sebastian Bach: The Learned Musician*, includes Christoph Bach's description of ten-year-old Sebastian's foundation for keyboard playing:

> The foundations for his playing of the clavier imply first and foremost the acquisition of a solid keyboard technique, involving the standard keyboard instruments, notably harpsichord and organ. On the organ, Bach needed to develop his technique with both hands and feet. Second,

he needed experience with the major keyboard genres and styles: improvisatory (for example, prelude and toccata) or strict (for example, fugue and ricercar); freely invented or based on a given subject or choral tune. Third, a musical foundation required familiarity with different approaches of individual composers.[15]

Improvising implies anything but drift. It implies direction, shape, coherence, and release. Every improviser needs to develop a bag of tricks at the keyboard. No doubt, as Schoenberg remarks, pianists in Beethoven's day had up their playing sleeves "a thorough supply of passagework by the yard, which they could snip off and use for any possible contingency." Yet, there remains for the improviser a dimension beyond tricks, moments of floating free, which Richard Powers so convincingly dramatizes.

Will asks his notation-bound friend, "You can't make it go on its own?"

The phrase "on its own" suggests a driving momentum as the player hears what is implied in the music being made and spins it out and away, lets it "float free." Next to this, one's normal level of acquaintance with the keyboard can seem marginal indeed.

What is it like to be inside that experience? The most radical description I've found so far comes from Karlheinz Stockhausen, describing his experience with "intuitive music." In rather homiletic terms, he likens a profound improvising experience to that of becoming selfless, like a radio receiver, or a medium.[16]

It is not a case of expressing oneself, he asserts, but of going beyond the limit of self, open to hear and release musical possibilities instantly intuited.

Whatever the inner dimensions of the improvising experience, it's clear to me that at a certain level improvising means giving up (or going beyond) the superficial level of control we amateurs have struggled so hard to acquire.

And letting go always involves risk.

The question arises: How have I been trained to see notation? How do I read it? Do I see it as closed? Open? What does it mean to see a text as open, not closed? Put another way, can I learn to read (hear) what is implied in the notation?

The question reminds me of a suggestion I sometimes offered when teaching beginning fiction writers as they tried to figure out how to intensify early versions of stories in which scenes, transitions, and characters finally seemed to be in place. Why was the story so lifeless? "Press your material," I urged. I knew perfectly well that on one level this directive made no sense. "Press the words, the sentences, the scenes for what lies behind them, what's not said, the iceberg that Henry James tells us lies beneath the surface. Look for implication. You may be surprised where this leads you. It will make you aware of possibilities hidden in the material. New directions, a whole new shape may emerge. Go with it."

My students had achieved one level of control. Now my advice was to loosen the control, look at the material another way. Relax with it. This urging occasionally helped them.

I decided to take the step. I called Julian Snow.

One full year into jazz improvisation lessons with a gifted teacher, I still lose my nerve when I reach the improv section of the tune I'm working on. Every day, I improvise over it differently, trying to put into practice what I'm learning about harmonic changes. I learn and drill the chord changes in the left hand, then figure out what might go with what so my right hand may learn to play over the keys with some semblance of interesting or pleasing sounds. Anxiety builds as lesson day approaches. I'm on my own this time, no class to protect me.

Has any music student ever gone to his or her lesson feeling fully prepared?

After we'd been through a number of tunes, worked on scales, triads, ways to alter chords, and so on, I decided to focus for a while on "Ain't Misbehavin'." I began by finding three tapes of Fats Waller playing the tune. I listened carefully, hearing what I could, then decided to limit my chord changes to one version. A small tape recorder sat beside me on the piano bench. I went stop-and-start for a long time, noting down what I could catch of Fats's transitions, his solo improvisations. To take in all his transitions would require more hours than I had, but I was able to identify some of his changes and his single-hand patterns, his licks. Of course I had to write this down. I am still far from being able to hear and retain without notation. I could also get the feel of the piece in his hands, his wonderful playfulness with the tune and with his listeners.

Then I had to work out my "rootless voicings." This turns out to be tough, for my fingers have grown accustomed to certain formations of chords more frequently found in eighteenth- and nineteenth-century classical music. For example, my fingers will pretty automatically go to the dominant seventh chords in basic keys, or to the tonic, or root, chord. A piano student's hands learn these formations very early.

To play "Ain't Misbehavin'" in a primitive stride style, on the downbeat I had to play the root or fifth of each chord with the left pinkie, then form a left-hand chord variously altered — by adding 6ths, 9ths, 11ths, 13ths, sharps, flats — to go with it. It took considerable time to form these chords, decide what sounded best in a given place, then go with it. With practice — back and forth, back and forth — my left hand had to grow quick at traveling these distances. Much of piano playing is about managing space quickly. Meanwhile, my right hand would play the melody against this and, in one section, simply improvise against it.

There were other considerations as I put this together: how one chord related to the next, what its function was as the whole piece moved forward, where the surprises came and why they were surprises, and how, finally, to get my hands comfortable with all this.

Ah, hands. Enter the drama of the hands.

How does it help me to know that Beethoven could hardly reach two tones above the octave, a tenth; that Rachmaninoff and Sviatoslav Richter could reach a twelfth; that Vladimir Horotitz's fingers were very long; and that Steinway build Josef Hoffman a special piano with narrower ivories to facilitate his reaching a ninth? Art Tatum would roll filberts around in his hands to increase their dexterity.[17]

These details fascinate me, but the problem is dealing with my hands, not the hands of others. In learning jazz improvisation, you become highly conscious of how your hands move around the keys. I look at these fingers trying to reach the F-sharp minor seventh in second inversion. I figure out ways to get there quickly from the preceding chord, and then on to the next. I work out mini exercises around these challenges, trying to get the feeling into my hands of making runs and chords. I give up and go chop celery for a salad.

Of course, beyond training finger / muscle memory, I need to understand what I'm doing. Week by week, I catch on to more. But like any skill, the test comes in putting what the brain is learning into the hand and fingers. So far, I still have to write out key sections of my arrangement. The improv section has to come together on the spot. I never write that out.

I drill on.

I have discovered that no one really knows the "proper" position at the piano or the optimum position for arm, wrist, or hand. In one course at the Peabody Institute, we watched a video of Vladimir Horowitz playing the Rachmaninoff Concerto No. 3 in D minor, op. 30.

He held his hands flat against the keys. Chopin, recognized as a wonderful teacher, felt piano students should begin their hand's acquaintance with the keyboard not with the scale of C, which is unnatural for the hand, but by placing the fingers on E-F#-G#-A#-B in order to begin with the most natural and comfortable position. His pupils spoke of how he tailored his advice about technique to the hands of each pupil. And we've all seen pictures of Glenn Gould's seemingly eccentric positioning at the piano.

So, in this regard, I feel free to experiment. It is absolutely lovely not to have a teacher saying, "Now please remember to hold your fingers as if you were holding an orange."

After "Ain't Misbehavin'" I moved on to learn another style of arranging a tune: open ballad style. I chose to work on "Stardust." Things got more complicated, partly my own doing. The four versions of "Stardust" I located in music books at the public library were all in the key of C. No sharps, no flats. Good. But Julian suggested I transpose it to another key, so I looked at ones we had covered so far. I had not yet worked in E major. Why not try that? My earnestness almost did me in.

In no time, my fingers were wandering in a forest of accidentals. I should have gone for flats, which I find easier than sharps. Thinking it might help, I hunted up something classical I had played in E major: the second movement from Beethoven's op. 90, a beautiful melody. I played through that a bit, then went back to Hoagy Carmichael. But Beethoven, in that Schubertian melody, let my fingers go the way they wanted to, for the most part. I somehow knew what to expect. Not so with my arrangement of Hoagy. The work of the fingers felt completely different there. I might be in the same key, but I was in a different order, facing a new kind of resistance in the hand. There was no ease to it.

I have now been working on "Stardust" for a month.

When you begin to look at a tune, think about its key, its scale, its triads, how to form appropriate altered chords, what type of song it is, and how you want it to sound — complications multiply. You start to notice new things. Tune becomes secondary. The changes are the thing.

My relationship to the keyboard has begun to change in

subtle ways. I am looking more at my hands and the keys, less at the page. And the keys themselves seem somehow different.

As I write these words, I have just come from about an hour and a half of working solely to get the chords of "Stardust" into my head and hands. This is complicated. In the A section, I am learning to play open ballad style, an entirely new configuration for the hands, at an opposite pole from stride. In the later repeat of the A section, I am going to move into a slow stride style. Instead of keeping my hands close together on the keyboard and moving them in sync, I now need differently shaped chords in my left hand, and I must be able to reach these quickly. The stride pattern in my left hand must become just about automatic. And then there is the right hand. I will resist the urge to write anything out for the improvisation. *Verboten.* As I think about what chords might go with the tune, for the first time I find myself actually grasping how the whole tone scale, the diminished scale, and the mixolydian scale might function here. Those alien mystifying words I've glanced at so often over the years — dorian, locrian, mixolydian — I have now actually begun to use. Never did I imagine that I would one day say, "Understanding the use of the mixolydian has made my day."

I have been writing fiction for over thirty years. Fiction writing is all about making it up. It is also about keeping going, persisting. When I turned to writing stories, I already knew the grammar and vocabulary of English. When I turned to improvising, I already knew some basic musical grammar and vocabulary.

Knowledge of English grammar and vocabulary does not immediately equip one to create a scene, suggest implication, shape a story, round out character, to say nothing of gradually growing more alert to the beautifully complex, verbal interrelationships that constitute a story. Writing demands patience.

An important step in story writing is reached when one begins to look beyond having the basic elements worked out and in place. When this threshold is crossed — if it is — the story comes to life. A fiction writer gets a second and a third and a fourth chance, a fiftieth chance to cross that threshold. Walk away from the heap of words, get some distance, return, look at it and hear it more critically. Cut. Shape. Consider the relationship of parts. Press for implication. Walk away from it again. Go eat some calories. (Don't call a friend.) Play the piano. Come back. Hear it as coming from someone else, from somewhere else. Become a reader.

Time is your friend.

Improvising is of the moment, a thing of now.[18] It comes into being, traces a shape, then dies. This is scary. Your musical sounds may describe a line, an arc, a question and answer, some other design. The analogy with words — phrase, sentence, paragraph — suggests itself.

Fiction writing, however, belongs to the world of notation. Improvising is writing in air, and writing in air is scary. There's nothing to show on paper. There are only sounds heard in the air. Fear of making a mistake glues us to the notes, makes us long for the consolation of text.

A few months ago, at a lesson, as I tried to improvise over the left hand chords of "What a Difference a Day Makes," I kept stopping, groaning, pausing. It sounded so messy. Finally I stopped altogether, feeling I couldn't, shouldn't, go on. I was murdering the piece.

Then came a few words from Julian on the difference between practice mode and performance mode. It's obvious, when you think about it. For practice mode, you work to get the notes perfect. In practice mode, I had been taping myself, listening each night to the previous day's efforts. Now I was in performance mode, where the imperative is to *keep going . . . do not stop . . . no matter what.*

"Mistakes," said Julian calmly, as I stopped groaning, "I make them all the time. The trick is to transform them into something else. Mistakes are opportunities. They can take you some place new. Seize the opportunity."

He sat down and improvised over the left hand harmonic progressions I had worked out. Then he deliberately sounded a jarring, distinctly unpleasant note, clearly, in context, "wrong." Quickly, in the next phrase, he restated the same "mistake" but contextualized it slightly differently so that it sounded like an interesting new pattern. He recontextualized with confidence. Suddenly the first "mistake" sounded intentional and downright intriguing.

"We need to be open to receive the great gift of mistakes," he said.

Transforming a fear of mistakes into a relish for risk is a tall order. The improviser is on a tightrope with no net. It happens in the instant, then disappears, floats away on air.

Can I manage, eventually, to play some classical music decently, even well, honor the integrity of texts, and also enjoy the freedom of improvising over popular music? Or even, now and then, over a bit of classical? So far I refuse to believe it must be either / or.

Perhaps this is one reason Richard Powers's novel touched me deeply. His narrator comes to understand the meeting of two different ways of musicking, different ways, one might say, of being in time, of searching out musical meaning, perhaps even of discovering new aspects of one's identity. Deep-rooted desire always signals something about who we are.

At long last, after lots of work, Joseph and Will fly together alongside one another at the keyboard.

"As long as our four hands kept moving," says Joseph, "the music for writing down and the music for letting loose found a way to share a nest."

Improvisation, like life itself, denies its creator the certitude of a predetermined path. Like life itself, its freedom is governed by limits as fundamental as the way a piano is tuned, the way a brain works. As I work out the musical framework for improvising, my fingers, my brain, my imagination, my background, my fears and hopes, my ear, my sense of adventure all play into the process, plus other things which no doubt I have yet to realize.

Here I am, embarking on yet another musical journey.

Never have I found an excursion into learning something new about music to be disappointing. The world of musicking is indeed a "bottomless place." Plumbing just one bit of that place excites me.

That a human being, at any age, can approach this "monster with iron in its heart," as one poet has called the piano, sit on a bench, raise poised hands over black and white ivory keys, press them, and send forth vibrations that sing and call and answer and complain and cry and rejoice and weep and speak beyond words will never cease to awaken wonder in me.

And after wonder comes curiosity.

How does one enter and move about in this strange, notationless cosmos of musicking? How does one elicit new and thrilling vibrations? How does one uncover musical sounds hiding beneath or beyond or around or above other musical sounds?

Who knows what music hides inside music already made?

Who knows what hides within the world we think we see and hear and touch and know?

I travel happily, haltingly, toward that revelation.

A Salute to Morning

The boys clattered out the door to music they probably would not otherwise ever hear.

A trill, *mezzo forte, con amore.*

My Chickering stood in the small book-lined room next to the front door. Some mornings, when the boys were little and busy gathering parkas, mittens, boots, and bookbags before heading out the door to different schools, my husband and I would manage to get to the piano and banjo. We would set up to play some peppy songs from the Twenties. The boys clattered out the door to music they probably would not otherwise ever hear. They clumped down the front steps — Tom off to French immersion, Andrew off to Special Education, as we plinked away at "Baby Face," "Bye Bye Blackbird," "Let's Do It," and other lively old songs. Echoes from my "Tiptoe Thru the Tulips" days.

Our conscious purpose was certainly not education. It was simply to put a fun musical ornament on a day about to unroll in its predictable way. We'd play for a few moments after they left, and then off went my husband to find his way into his own particular heart of educational darkness; up I went to the third floor room to improvise my way into yet another fictional character's libretto.

Yet, the trill — it sent a little vibration, an upbeat tremolo through the hours that followed, an antidote to winter in a world that often felt claustrophobic.

Better than a pill.

Bells in China

As the robed musicians make their eerie, disturbing, oddly beautiful, sometimes deeply sonorous sounds, they send forth tones strong, sweet, or stridently dissonant to lead this wandering tourist into an alien, intriguing world.

When memory's tiny flicks unexpectedly connect, we sometimes say, "That rings a bell."

And so, the sound of the bells I meet in Wuhan, capital of Hubei Province in China, ring memory bells: convent bells telling us to stop or start whatever we were supposed to be doing; bells calling us to prayer; bells summoning kids home as dusk turned toward dark; church bells tolling for Sunday Mass in Sackville, New Brunswick, as son Andrew proudly pulled the rope; and I, Andrew's mother, feeling oh so monastic many years ago as I pulled the long rope to toll the heavy Angelus Bell at noon to signal remembrance of an angel appearing to Mary. Even Marcel Proust felt the power of bells when the sudden unexpected sound of the garden bell from Combray led him back and back and back through tangled pathways toward his great work of discovery through remembering.

The power of these bells triumphs over the Shanghai neon

and traffic glut I've just left behind, over the thrum of sixteen million humans walking and hawking, of stone dragons breathing fire, of child acrobats daring death. Golden Buddhas have glared at me in jewel-encrusted rage, the silk worm has performed, but no performance has yet topped these bells.

Having descended from the spot at the Yellow Crane Pavilion where Wang Zian, the Taoist priest, set off on a yellow crane to become one of the immortals, we mortals are headed out of town.

We are headed for the Provincial Museum, a delay on our way to embark and cruise the Yangtze.

"Time here is limited," our guide cautions as we climb off the bus. "You can go directly into the museum to view rare objects excavated from the tomb of Marquis Yi of Zeng, or you may go to the musical presentation in the theater. It's about to begin."

I hurry into the theater.

On the stage in a straight row sit ten musicians in brilliant white, turquoise, and red silk gowns. They must be silk; I have just seen the worms at work. On their laps or held up to their mouths are various instruments I cannot name, some of which I will later read about in the museum.

Behind the musicians, arranged in ascending height, stand reproductions of the massive, magnificent hand-crafted bronze bells. I'll view the actual bells later in the museum, along with 125 musical instruments unearthed in this tomb: stone chimes, drum, 25-string zither, lo-string zither, Jun zhong (5-string pitch tuner), Sheng, pipe, and bamboo flute, plus 1,000 pieces of instrument accessories. A whole musicological system is inscribed on the bells and stone chimes dating from 500 B.C.E. For this moment, though, it's the bells.

Each great stone bell produces two different tones when struck. As the robed musicians make their eerie, disturbing, oddly beautiful, sometimes deeply sonorous sounds, they send forth tones strong, sweet, or stridently dissonant to lead this wandering tourist into an alien, intriguing world. Behind the musicians, whose fingers pluck what must be zithers, a turquoise robed figure glides from bell to bell, pulling music from their five-and-a-half octave range.

Later I learn that the middle three bells produce twelve semitones each and can be modulated. The law of ranges is C major, playing music of a five-, six-, or seven-note scale.

I don't need any of this information to hear what I now hear. Moving tones breathe out toward us, sustained by a deep, full, round sound from struck bells that says: We shall last forever, our vibrations enter the universe and will remain there, invisible, eternally sounding.

Who knows what musical and nonmusical meaning attached to these ancient, immense, hand-crafted bells excavated from the tomb of Marquis Yi Zeng, which dates to 433 B.C.E., the time of "Warring States," the peak of bronze casting technology, and obviously, one high point of an elaborately developed instrument technology and musical theory in ancient China.

I do not "get" the pitches, harmonies, resolutions (if they exist) of Chinese music. I listen with minimal connection. The one CD I bought strikes me as rearranged to fit diatonically conditioned Western ears. We can, however, expand our ear's capacity. I've worked at that through jazz improvisation. Here in Wuhan a new musical world meets me: time travel through bell tones. Folks were busy in Athens in the fifth century B.C.E., but they were busy here in Wuhan as well.

I'm a bit sorry when — sop to tourists' ears — they conclude with the melody from Beethoven's Ninth, "Ode to Joy." An experience of alien sounds can be cathartic.

What has Marquis Yi of Zeng to do with me?

Everything and nothing. His buried bells and instruments created a fascinating interlude that sent tones through me more speaking than the elaborate histrionics of the Peking Opera, more beguiling than the canned Chinese music played for tourists wandering the jade factory, more colorful than the flowing sleeve arabesques of minority dancers in Guilin. His bells sing of buried worlds beneath the earth we traverse, we tourists in our walking shoes.

Watch where you step.

Next comes a scurry through the museum to see the real bells. Huge, covered by intricate geometric designs, they display 164 elegantly threatening dragons. My hastily jotted notes tell me that ornamentation of this period included casting, gold-inlaying, and decorating techniques of round shape sculpture, relief, intaglio, and painting. The hunger of the imagination and the powers of the hand ornament these instruments.

The 3,755 inscriptions on the bells, supports, and hangers record events, the sound each bell makes, and musical theories such as number, note names, scale notes, octaves, and relations of pitch.

And so I have wandered into a strange musical resurrection drama silently presented here in the museum and aurally in the theater, another joining of ear and eye and hand, from original castor and welder to the graceful hands of performers to please the casual tourist or the musically curious. For me, this imagined journey over centuries "rings a bell." The nameless medieval monk who applied black squares of chant to vellum cast his shadow forward through time, as did the hands that created, embellished, and sounded these wondrous bells.

After this will come more famous and hyped Chinese wonders: the Yangtze, the Great Wall, the buried Terra Cotta soldiers — all memorable. Yet especially did this hour at the provincial theater and museum in Wuhan ornament a conventional tourist route and feed my own hungering imagination. In homage to the ancient Marquis (who knows his cruelties or benevolence?), all these musical instruments, this testimony to civilization was buried in his vast tomb, preserved intact, dug up, presented to later eyes and ears from across the globe.

Music conquers distance.

Continuities play through variations.

Did the Marquis play an instrument or simply listen?

An Evening at the Piano

Now is the time for free-wheeling play. It's a kind of excitement you wish everyone could enjoy. Raiding the cookie jar of possibility. Trying and tasting. It's not about seeking perfection tonight, it's about exploring.

You hoist high the heavy lid, relish its weight in your hands, the pressure that tightens your arm muscle and wrist. Your left hand, meanwhile, extracts the long stick from its groove in the piano and lifts it to find the hole on the underside of the lid. Then, with care, you ease the heaviness down to its resting place.

Ah, there they lie exposed — gleaming golden strings. A subtle ping of excitement that began with lifting the lid races through you. This is a sexy moment.

Most often, you play with the lid down or propped open on the short stick, strings just partly visible. Not tonight.

Tonight, their vibrations will ring out through the whole house.

Not even triple fortissimo will distract your husband, in another room behind two closed doors, bent over his crossword puzzle. No children sleeping upstairs to worry about either.

Let it ring!

Possibility gleams in those shining, mute strings. The house is quiet. You have time, God's gift. You have this wondrous instrument, Mr. Steinway's gift. Who knows what may emerge?

Sheet music and albums lie about untidily — on the coffee table, on the floor beside the piano bench — leftovers from hours snatched here and there throughout the week. What is your mood? Indeterminate. You'll let yourself be taken into terrain and weather unknown, yet sometimes oddly familiar, whichever way the strange black code on those lined pages leads you. There is no one here to listen, to judge, except you, and you intend to keep that critical critter at bay tonight.

Jelly Roll Morton stares up at you from the album cover near your feet. He's due back at the public library in three days. Maybe you'll entertain yourself by sight-reading a rag later. And there, next to the music rack on the piano, lies Liszt's Consolation No. 3 in D-flat Major, purchased after you heard Horowitz play it on a CD and thought, "Now there's something by Liszt I could play!" His transcriptions of Beethoven's symphonies have satisfied and stymied you, but his fantasies on opera remain beyond reach. Keep him nearby, just in case you need consolation later from that tormented monk. And then there's a jazz fake book, the sixth edition of *The Real Book*, peeking out from under Jelly Roll. Keep that on the floor there too. In an hour or so, the urge may strike to abandon the old guys. For now, though, go rummage through the too low music cabinet over there at the end of the piano. It holds the "Greats."

You kneel before it and open its doors to rainbow piles of music. Fish through to your heart's content. What guides your hands, moves you to pull out some, leave others behind? The desire of the moment, simply that.

Here's Chopin in his yellow G. Schirmer overcoat: etudes, nocturnes. Pull them out. The evening would be incomplete without Chopin. No Bach tonight, thank you. And leave aside

Schubert's sonatas, also in their shiny red cover. His "heavenly lengths" would keep you here till midnight. Push past the pale green Mozart for four hands and the darker green Bischoff edition of Bach's partitas. It's the thin red album you're after, Beethoven's bagatelles, the Wiener Urtext Edition. Here you are in the Land of Ur. Pass by various albums for four-hand playing — Brahms, Beethoven, Schubert, Dvôrák. These are for another day with your partner Gretchen. They spell work.

That pale yellow sheet music, yes. Pull it out! Paderewski's Nocturne, op. 16, no. 4, remains one of your returned-to treasures, ever since you tracked it down after hearing it played as an encore. And here are three old Haydn sonatas you worked on. Can it be? About sixty years ago with Professor Bonn? Remnants of grammar school industriousness. There is his shaky writing telling you to notice a diminished chord, a dominant seventh. Pull it out. Surely some of it remains in muscle memory.

It's a romp, this rummaging, a romp through possibility and a seizing through sudden desire. And all the while, as you poke and pick, that tremor of excitement pings away inside.

Back at the piano, the pile is beside you on the bench and some on the floor. You've set the album of Hoagy Carmichael aside, and over on the coffee table where you can almost reach them are the two thick volumes of Beethoven's sonatas.

You have time. Nothing that smacks of work is allowed tonight. Your half-finished arrangement of "Stardust" can wait till tomorrow. You still have four days before Thursday's lesson. And don't go near Mozart, either, for tomorrow you'll hear your favorite pianist, Stephen Hough, play a Mozart piano concerto at an open rehearsal of the Oregon Symphony. Once again, his *pianissimo* will stun your heart into breath-stopping stillness.

Now is the time for free-wheeling play. It's a kind of excitement you wish everyone could enjoy. Raiding the cookie jar of possibility. Trying and tasting. It's not about seeking perfection tonight, it's about exploring. You'll aim to hit the right notes but often will miss. That's okay, this is just for fun.

You remember calling upstairs to an invisible child, dangerously quiet, and asking, "What're you doing?" The answer often came, "Jes playin'."

You are jes playin'.

I open the Chopin etudes, mentioned yesterday to me by a friend who is currently struggling with one. I flip through, find three that I have tackled at some point in the distant past. They will be only partially in my fingers now. Doesn't matter. I play through them, savoring sounds still familiar, dear, with enough correct notes that my hands feel fairly comfortable, pausing for accidentals here and there. Some snares never disappear, though, unless you work persistently at them. I pause, study, puzzle out one complex chord with each note both sharped and flatted. Now this is perverse. I remember stopping here many times. Still, op. 25, no. 7 seduces me again with that gorgeous bass melody, rising, falling, its plaintive full tone in the left hand singing something piercingly sad and hopeful. It makes me want to stop and get it right.

From a perfectionist's point of view and perhaps from a teacher's, my procedure is heretical. I simply play along, don't over-worry mistakes.

A while later, past some more Chopin and that beloved Paderewski nocturne, I see near my feet the music for *My Fair Lady*. I must have bought it a long time ago on impulse, maybe after seeing Rex Harrison in the movie. It looks untouched. Now and then I've found a lead sheet in a fake book and played one of my favorites, "I've Grown Accustomed to Her Face" or "I Could Have Danced All Night," but I've never seen these arrangements. In a week or so, I'll be seeing *My Fair Lady* for the first time on stage. Now, with great delight, I play through all these songs. Lerner and Loewe sing and dance in my living room, the tunes come alive as I try to put to use some things I've recently learned about chord progressions, the diminished scale, rootless voicings. But this begins to feel too much like work. Onward.

It's the absence of aiming for perfection that makes this such fun. Such a release.

And then I cannot resist. It's an urge that comes over me frequently — those two thick books of Beethoven there on the coffee table. I'll have to dip into them before I quit. As I said, I can't resist.

Last summer, I discovered Charles Rosen's *Piano Notes*.[19] His discussion of the limited familiarity a typical music student has with the vast piano repertoire surprised me. It also cheered me. Rosen asserted that in eight hours one could read through all the Schubert sonatas. Then he claimed that about six months of sight-reading daily for three hours could send one through most of the keyboard music of Bach, Handel, Mozart, Chopin, Schumann, Mendelssohn, and Brahms. He went on to estimate the hours required for sight-reading Haydn, Debussy, Ravel, Schoenberg, Stravinsky, von Webern, and Berg.

I don't have all that time. I love to sight-read.

So I made a decision. I would spend the summer reading through the thirty-two Beethoven sonatas. An absurd ambition, for I have formally studied only two or three, decades ago, and the rest I've just picked at according to the mood. Still, I did not intend to pine over impossibility. Besides, I have plenty of music already on my summer plate: serious preparation for at least two hours a week of practice with my partner to polish a little recital of Dvořák's *Legenden* for indulgent friends; learning a few banjo pieces with my husband; preparing for a weekly lesson in jazz improvisation; and working to perfect a couple of classical pieces I still had to choose.

Even so, I resolved to tackle the Beethoven, and my terms were clear. I would not try to get them anywhere close to tempo. I would not agonize over mistakes. I would persist, though I knew I would eventually hit impossibility.

Three things fortified me. First, a passionate desire to know more about Beethoven, stimulated by a course about his music that I took the first year I retired from teaching. Taught by a brilliant pianist, Jean-David Coen, these classes fed a latent hunger in me and enlarged my understanding when he would, on the spot, illustrate his point at the piano.

Second, my Beethoven appetite was further fed during a week I spent at the Peabody Institute of Music studying Beethoven concertos, symphonies, and sonatas under Michael Habermann. To hear Habermann go to the piano and articulate Beethoven's squalls and serenities was a revelation. His ready talent stunned the class. In addition to that, his refined musical insight into those sonatas left me more deeply drawn to my impossible goal. I have kept my notes from both courses and, of an evening now and then, have pulled them out to buoy up my efforts with a sonata.

My third resource was CDs of Schnabel playing the sonatas, so I could combine playing with listening.

I read the sonatas as slowly as necessary. In days of teaching Joyce's *Ulysses*, did we not take time over a page, a paragraph? In years of composing stories, did I not allow hours to stare at piles of words and try to sense their implications, their possibilities? So I read the notes slowly, sometimes at a snail's pace. This was not an exercise in perfection; I was moving into those sounds, exploring them, facing the impossible demands on my hands, realizing the expanding dimensions of the keyboard during Beethoven's lifetime, eventually having to face the looming wall of my inadequacies as a sight-reader and pianist. There were many mini-walls, parts I had to skip over, but I finally hit the impassable one at op. 106, no. 29, "Hammerclavier," as we call it. Thereafter, I simply listened, sometimes score in hand.

It was a challenging, thrilling, stimulating trip. I came upon new vistas, discovered whole continents, survived capsizings, drownings, vanishings, near-death experiences, recoveries. To discover that I could do more that I'd thought cast a certain healing glow on the whole effort.

I hope some day to repeat that journey.

Sometimes, on a sight-reading evening or during the Beethoven excursion, I would stop, look carefully, and wonder, "What is he doing? How does he get this effect?" Sometimes, I don't want to stop or analyze, so I just go on rippling or limping along, sending music out into space, sensing the melodic line, hearing it, listening for interesting harmony, feeling what I can as I try to make music.

Who of us has not known anticipation that comes when you feel the heft of an about-to-be-read book in your hands, one you've been waiting to read. The weight is part of it, the size, and then the parting of the covers. Thereafter comes the careful, curious turning of the title page, the dedication. Then you dive in.

This is the pull of reading. You are there alone with the book, its pages, its words. One after the other, those black characters on white draw you forward, feed a foretaste of pleasure, frustrate your expectations, answer your yearnings, offer you secrets. I speak here primarily of reading fiction. It is commonplace to observe that many structures of classical music in the Western tradition emulate the dramatic form of anticipation and delay, of crisis, resolution, tension and release. My point is not to belabor that, but simply to indicate that something of the same excitement and thrill emerges from an evening of reading music. The piece may be fresh, as with a new book, or familiar, as with one read again to recapture an earlier pleasure. For even if you have looked at the music before, that may have been long ago, and worlds have intervened. The page before you — dense with black notes, accidentals, marking for tempo, coded dynamics, all those *ff*s and *pp*s, all those Italian or German words — asks that you become a sight-reader again.

You are both an explorer, ready to lead and be led, and

an audience, ready to listen and to hear. You are a charmer, calling forth from gleaming strings vibrations that send intricate pitch patterns pulsing through the house. You are a channeler, a reader. You are two hands, ten fingers, touching designs into black and white ivory that send hammers toward strings that sing into the air of an empty room the mystery of scale and triad. You are body and instrument, memory and mind, decoder and music maker. You are playing the piano.

REUNION

No life is comprised of a single story. Yet, passing years intensify one's desire to trace some lines of meaning in your own story. Patterns emerge, sighting of lost chances, adjustment of angles toward understanding oneself and others. So it is that time's passing changes our perspectives on our own past.

These are not prison bars through which I peer. Nor are those singing beside me, behind me, with me — crowded into this small space next to the organ, their shoulders rubbing mine, their tones harmonizing with mine — prisoners.

The occasion is my fiftieth reunion at the College of New Rochelle.

No trip is single in its layers, and I discover this one to be densely layered, the consequence, perhaps, of living seven decades plus, traversing several worlds, pondering how they relate, and spending years of delight and torment within this very setting as a student and, later, as a nun.

Time passes. Layers deepen.

For the returned alumna, a college reunion invites a meshing of past experience and present seeing. It may, as well, awaken surges of feeling, unexpectedly fresh after decades of life lived differently elsewhere. It's a return to a place of friendships, personal exploration, discoveries, decisions. For some, such a return may generate a deepened sense of how closely bound are comedy and pain in the theater of life. In addition to all this, for me it meant returning to the site where I clarified a defining choice of my life.

Conclusions I do not seek here. Recognition is enough. In both first experience and return, light is mottled with shadow. All seeing, then and now, is partial, and there remains for me, even now, a value in having decided to return. No life is comprised of a single story. Yet, passing years intensify one's desire to trace some lines of meaning in one's story. Patterns emerge, sighting of lost chances, adjustment of angles toward understanding oneself and others. So it is that time's passing changes our perspectives on our own past. Experiencing profound loss is only part of any life story.

In his *Spiritual Exercises*, St. Ignatius of Loyola aims to teach us how to meditate. He urges the retreatant to begin by creating a "composition of place." Call forth in your imagination a scene from the life of Jesus. Place yourself in that scene. See its details, its setting, its characters. Listen to them, follow their actions, feel their feelings. Then, he counsels, conclude your meditation with a resolution about your own life in relation to the import of the scene.

I offer here three compositions of place: chapel, castle, ballroom. A unifying spirit breathes through them, created by the past itself or by my memory of that past recreated in this present.

Can they lead to any resolution?

CHAPEL

The organ is silent. We are singing a cappella: "O Esca Viatorum," "O Food of Wayfarers." My hymn sheet identifies our composer as Enrico Jsaak (1498). As my lips frame these wonderful open vowels, *O Esca Viatorum, O Panis Angelorum,* I can peer out to the left, at a sharp angle, and see the crowded front pews. A world changed utterly.

I look past our graceful, bright-eyed director, Sister Beth, in her light linen jacket and darker slacks. As an undergraduate I knew her simply as Beth, always filled with music, a singing presence, a woman who entered the Order a few years after me. She lives a life dedicated to music, bringing the joy of song to hundreds of young students in Westchester County and New England through her work in schools and in her summer music camp. By no external sign would you label her "Sister." Changed, but not utterly.

Straight ahead of me on the far side of the sanctuary, I see the seated Capuchin priest whose overly long homily flew right by me.

Out in the chapel proper, facing the altar glorious in gold for this one-hundredth anniversary of the college's founding, rows of women and men listen to our singing. Or perhaps they, too, are elsewhere, thinking of decreasing dividends or erectile dysfunction or this month's Visa bill.

This rainy weekend in New Rochelle we honor the first Catholic women's college in the state of New York, founded in 1904. Today's Mass offers a different approach to articulating shared belief. For the words of the Credo, the Capuchin substituted words from the renewal of baptismal vows at the Easter Vigil, the solemn liturgical celebration of Christ's resurrection. He left out Satan entirely, thank heaven.

Instead, we sang the last three questions from that part of the liturgy, asking if we believe in Jesus, the Son, the Father and Creator, and the Holy Spirit.

After each question, we invited the congregation out in front to sing the following:

> If you believe and I believe
> And we together pray,
> The Holy Spirit must come down

And set God's people free,
And set God's people free,
And set God's people free,
The Holy Spirit must come down
And set God's people free.

The responsory is, I later learn, a Zimbabwean derivative of an old English folk melody arranged by John L. Bell. The introductory "if" says it all. It is unimaginable that, in 1904, the intrepid Mother Irene Gill would have sung such words at the founding of this college. One might quibble now about how we identify "God's people," and how easily we sing "must," but for today's liturgy, that plea to be set free seems a new and refreshing strength singing out in the old chapel.

Directly across from us singers, separated from the sanctuary by vertical wooden palings that match those framing our smaller space here, lies the nuns' transept. As an undergraduate, I would come into the vacant chapel at odd times, sit in a pew, and just listen to the eerie, pleasing, mysterious chanting of the Divine Office emanating from there. The nuns were invisible to me, but their voices, raised in praise, echoing through the emptiness, hinted at spaces and realities far beyond the finite bindings of time. I didn't know what they chanted, but it lifted me out of the moment.

Now, over there, I see rows of cushioned chairs angled to face the altar. The chairs are empty today; all able-bodied nuns are out in the chapel pews mingling with their alumnae. On other days, these cushions support aging, dedicated bones.

As I round my vowels and sing of angels, even empty chairs can call up ghosts.

One not-yet-so-fragile nun was my novice mistress almost fifty years ago. She was energetic enough then to lay out in crisp tones the steps of our chosen path up the ladder of spiritual perfection, steps of penance and prayer that would lead us nuns-in-training to a closer union with God. My classmates here today would remember her primarily as New

Rochelle's dean of discipline, feared dispenser of demerits. As their student body president, how often I confronted her imperturbability as I argued for the students' point of view.

Two months after graduation I entered the Order. By an odd turn of events, a year after that, this former dean of discipline and professor of math was transferred from the college to Beacon, New York, out in the woods, to take on the heavy responsibility of training us novices for religious life. Suddenly, the figure who had countered my push for student freedoms was now, in a different setting, giving us novices a daily class in prayer, noting our violations of the rule, encouraging us along the way to deeper silence and prayer. Actually, I now remember her most for updating the novitiate plumbing when she arrived so that we earnest mortifiers of the body could have more than one bath a week. She brought into our lives the bliss of the evening shower, an imperfect bliss, to be sure, as we first had to kill any wayward garter snakes on the cellar shower floor. Even so, after hours of kneeling upright in chapel and then gardening in heavy black robes in high humidity came the blessed relief of water pouring on hot, tired, mortified flesh.

Another cushion must also now support my former superior here who, during my four years as a religious in this particular house, was in no way a friend. Darkness arises here. Even today I think of her as an adversary and hope our paths do not cross. This woman did not teach at the college. As students we never saw her, for she lived and moved within the castle where many of the religious lived. We knew only those nuns teaching in the classroom or functioning as corridor mothers in the dorms. She did neither. Nine years later, when I returned to this community no longer a mere student but now as a teacher, corridor mother, and professed Ursuline, our relationship as superior and subject grew strained. I came to feel her effect on those bound to obey her will was damaging to spirit and mind. For the most part, as superior and subject for four years until I departed for Cornell, we sustained cautious civility.

Tonight will feature a grand dinner in the castle. Should

she and I meet, politeness will prevail. There is no point in exploring this bit of my past with my classmates. It would sound like a fairy tale of a wolf in sheep's clothing.

It was no fairy tale.

Right now, looking at empty choir stalls over in the transept, I wonder how many dear old nun friends have vacated their cushioned chairs to float around with the angels of whom we sing. How those old choir stalls with their small kneelers challenged us young nuns to balance on them and kneel upright, not slip into self-coddling by leaning back to rest on the tiny shelf seat so tantalizingly close behind us. These days, the era of piously callused knees seems to have ended.

O panis angelorum,
O manna coelitum,
Esurientes ciba . . .

The bread of angels sharing,
O Manna from on high!
We hunger; Lord, supply us . . .

We sing to express, to celebrate, and, above all, to awaken memory — in this case, the memory of years of early morning Mass with liturgy sung by choir members, some stumbling into chapel with pj's hidden beneath black choir gowns. I was not a choir member, but usually a daily Mass attender, as my college roommate reminded me at dinner last night: "Remember how you would tap me on the shoulder and ask if I wanted to get up for Mass? I'd grunt and roll over."

Only much later would I realize how extraordinary it was for a college choir in the Fifties to sing not only the Ordinary of the Mass each day — the Kyrie, Gloria, Credo, Sanctus, Agnus Dei — but also the changing proper for each day, and often, at the Offertory, include a polyphonic number. Each morning the choir offered our ears liturgical pearls of rare beauty.

Dulcedine non priva
Corda quarentium.

Nor thy delights deny us,
Whose hearts to thee draw nigh.

Ours is an assembly today of women, men, nuns, seculars, older, younger, poorer, richer, nicked, scarred, traumatized, sorrowful, joyful, or somewhere in between. For one weekend, differences are buried or on hold: political party, divorces, abortions, adulteries, wars, poverty, riches, disability, violence, education, taxes, despair.

Do not deprive of sweetness the hearts of the seeking ones.

Every one of us lives in the crack between longing for what we see as possible and surviving what is.

Quarentium.

It may be that Catholic women's education of the Fifties engendered in susceptible hearts and souls a longing for transcendence in some form: to see the face of God.

I am conditioned from my pious mother's womb to expect not an answer, but at least a hearing, an "ear," somewhere "up there," above our earthly palings. Addressing God implies this. Our hymn here speaks in the vocative, addresses God in poetically veiled forms.

On the rood beam over the sanctuary entrance, Mary and Joseph stand beneath the crucified Christ and above the inscription "Greater Love Than This No Man Hath."

Many years ago, on New Year's Eve in 1965, out in the aisle between the pews near the front of this chapel, I lay in my habit on those stones, prostrate at midnight, fireworks faintly audible in the snow-covered distance outside, praying to know if my perception of irreducible contradictions built into my experience of religious life after following its discipline faithfully for years was deluded, was valid. And if valid, how could I still affirm that way? How could I go on wearing the habit, living in community, bearing witness to something I could no longer believe in?

Quarentium.

An hour or so ago, as Mass was about to begin, responding to Beth's inviting eye and her beckoning hand, I climbed over my neighbors' knees, left my pew in the main chapel and came forward, crossing the very spot on the stones where I had lain all those years ago. To the right of the sanctuary, I came through the entrance to this choir space where I had once played the organ. What drew me from the crowded pew, from remaining outside? Why did I come forward to this spot where now I could face the sanctuary from a new angle, look across at the nuns' transept where I had chanted the Hours daily for four years?

I wanted to sing. Just that. Wanted to harmonize. So I joined my sister wayfarers.

CASTLE

Later in the day, our evening path leads us to the center of campus, a true castle, crenellated gray stone turrets rising high above the handsome three story building.

We, the Golden Jubilee Class, have gathered inside the castle in two high-ceilinged parlors once reserved for annual benefactors' teas, off-limits to us students. Round tables clothed in white fill both rooms: our servers wear black and white. The occasional old nun in pastel tones floats about greeting those she knew back then.

Here comes my old novice mistress of the blessed showers, with her wrinkled, still pixie-ish face, her old back-and-white habit exchanged for a dark blue suit, her nun's name changed back to her original baptismal name. Many nuns returned to baptismal names when changes after Vatican II finally trickled down into the ranks. All smiles, our pixie nun comes toward us, remembering each name fifty years later. Should I say "Thank you for the shower?" My classmates know of the novitiate regimen only what they read in fashionable fiction. Sister Mary Ignatius doesn't begin to tell all. Nunsense is nonsense.

We embrace loosely. She once gave a talk to us novices that likened the spiritual life to a pie — this portion prayer, this portion good works, and I forget the third portion. I can still picture the trisected circle she chalked on the blackboard as we took careful notes.

She floats away.

I could liven up this moment.

"Over there," I could say, "near the table at the far end of this room, we were laid out when dead. No flowers. Dark room. Just a box and beside it tall beeswax tapers. Two nuns kept watch all night before the funeral."

Just keep quiet. *Six Feet Under* suffices for TV funeral entertainment these days. No need to elaborate here on convent funeral practices.

♪ ♪

Castle: a place designed to protect those inside from the enemy, the outsider.

The metaphor of war is familiar to any Christian. St. Paul is full of it. "Put on the armor of salvation." "Endure hardship as a good soldier of Jesus Christ." Many saints, Ignatius among them, himself born to a noble soldiering family and a castle, waged war against their own Evil Axis: the world, the flesh, and the devil. Even the psalms celebrate victories in battle, bashings of heads against rock. As high school students we belted out our Catholic Action song:

> An army of youth flying the standard of truth
> Is fighting for Christ the Lord;
> Heads lifted high, Catholic action our cry
> And the cross our only sword!

More profoundly, St. Teresa of Avila likened the innermost place of encounter with God to an interior castle.

Past cocktails, we sit at our round table — to my left, Fran, wife of G. Gordon Liddy, to my right the physician husband of my roommate. How novel to slice my steak and chat with a male in this inner sanctum. The last male I encountered here was a priest. In the nearby dining room, I served him breakfast, but did not eat with him.

There is no getting inside another's castle, any more than we can know what lies beneath the earth on which we tread, what lies behind the images of life we see and think we can decode. And so, part of me, relishing the company, the steak, the orderly graciousness of these rooms, part of me wanted to proclaim.

"Here, in and around this castle, I moved into darkness. Here I came to suspect that, as they were evolving in the early Sixties, the Ursulines, perhaps along with many other Orders, were losing their way. Caught in the ferment of the Second Vatican Council, our way of viewing the world, ourselves, eternity, our place in all this, grew wobbly. How could an Order dedicated to education be refusing to let its sisters read certain books? Someone — one of my students in English? — sneaked me a thirty-five cent copy of *Lady Chatterley's Lover* hidden inside a cover for Shakespeare's *As You Like It*. That little comic treasure has survived periodic purgings of my bookshelves.

"And how could it be," I wondered back then, "that in following Jesus, who ate with reprobates and mingled with lepers and asked the Samaritan woman for drink, who washed his disciples' feet and submitted to Magdalen's ministrations, how could it be that we were so rigorously trained to suspect evil in any human touch? Why did the Order institutionalize human distance as so desirable? We were not to touch one another's fingers as we passed vegetable dishes at table. Friendship with men was suspect. Contradictions large and small multiplied in the life as I then experienced it. Today we live in a world beset by weapons of mass destruction and ingenious ways of linking God and death. Yet spiritual weapons of mass destruction still bear thinking about. Were we really, by our lives, bearing witness to the incarnation of God in this troubled and needy world?"

I uttered none of this.

What held me back? As I write now, the question arises again: what kept me silent? I had rich fodder to mine for appreciative giggles. What kept me merely sociable and pleasant in the midst of these layers of humor and irony that might have entertained friends my age who had shared the college years?

What point would it have served?

It might amuse. It might surprise. It could easily bore.

Besides, why go heavy in such a setting? I could have stayed away. No: I had chosen to return to the reunion. Tangled and deep strands of affection course through our lives. I still had good friends of many years here, nuns who had shared an important part of my life, friends who had shared earlier student years on this campus.

Let those values stand.

In those moments at dinner, it simply felt impossible to convey with any clarity, in telling detail, what I was feeling. Certainly, each of these at my table carried their own shadows. So as I sat at the table in the long parlor that night soothed by harp melodies coming from a nearby room, disguised by my rayon Hawaiian print with its side slits, brightened by my discreet Clinique blush, I did not stand and shout "Listen to what it was really like here." There would be no point. The felt situation seemed too complex, too remote and simultaneously too present. I did not want to reduce my whole experience to a joke.

Many years would pass before I would try here to spread out in words this mesh of memory in its layers and tangled threads. With the advantage of distance in time and space, I make this attempt now, reminded by Kafka in the quotation above my desk: "The right perception of any matter and a misunderstanding of the same matter do not wholly exclude each other."

I enjoyed the meal. *Esca viatorum.*

Delicious.

I enjoyed the conversation, encountering faces many years unseen. Ours was a small class: 140. I knew them all.

The harp played on.

BALLROOM

A ballroom offers promise of release and a time for dress-up, assuming one has found a pleasing partner and has learned basic steps. In bygone college days, it offered the nuns a chance to tuck a little tulle into offending necklines. Maura Ballroom, with its golden wooden floor, its slightly raised stage at the far end, and its rows of fancy chairs with curved legs lining the side walls, was built in 1912. Filled with light, it extended behind closed glass doors beneath one end of the dormitory, promising us pleasure after term papers, deadlines, demerits, and discipline.

Lester Lanin needed no amplifying at the Sophomore Cotillion. How could that popular bandleader — who played for presidential inaugurations and would serenade Grace Kelly at her engagement party and Prince Charles and Lady Diana at their wedding — how could he guess what a tempest his rhythms set off in the teapot of our Sophomore Cotillion as his orchestra worked its compelling magic? Mickey, stunning in her billowing dress, danced the Hula Ha. Round and round. We clapped. Faster. Faster. The ballroom grew electric. Hiking up our ball gowns, we climbed up on those golden chairs, the better to see, little Lester Lanin hats perched on our hairdos.

We twisted our hips with glee, clapping, clapping, oh, the fun of it, the release. From a small balcony above one end of the room, nuns kept watch. These were hardly the cultural traits the college catalogue promised we would exhibit after years of Ursuline education.

Did anyone spot, on the sidelines, our class advisor sporting a look of consternation?

We were much too busy dancing, jumping down from the chairs, joining in the Hula Ha, bounding about in abandon.

Did anyone notice that class advisor approach the chaperone, a father, and ask him to do something?

We went on dancing — raucous, out of control — as we were told the next morning in solemn assembly. A disgrace.

CODA

Next day, Sunday, I was scheduled to leave by train at one o'clock.

After one more reunion event, a large brunch, I wandered off alone to pack up my things and call a cab.

On the path behind the castle refectory, I passed the large campus cross on its round grassy island. I paused.

Suddenly, beautiful singing floated from the chapel.

I could not resist.

So I veered left, passed the *Ulmus silens,* which had bidden decades of students to hush before entering chapel. I opened the heavy outside door, paused a moment, climbed the winding stone staircase, and entered chapel.

I stood way in back, looking, listening.

The chapel was half full. Sister Helen, a college classmate who had joined the Carmelite Order, caught sight of me and motioned me to come sit with her, about two pews from the back.

We knelt for the Communion. The rows started to approach the altar. I joined them.

Esca viatorum.

I turned back from the Communion rail to come down

the side aisle, the dry taste of the wafer and the faintly sweet residue of altar wine still in my mouth. I passed faces I had known in another, earlier life, singing, praying, heads down or up, eyes closed or open. A group of nuns was sitting together. I caught the eye of a couple of old friends, winked at one, waved to another, and continued down the aisle, out the chapel door, down the hollowed stone stairs, through the outer door, past the *Ulmus silens*, and veered left down another path toward the dorm.

And then it came: unexpected, unfathomable, rising from depths I could not name, the moment that signaled the end to reunion. I hesitate to include it here, yet somehow it belongs. From what source did those tears arise? It went beyond loss, beyond sadness, beyond control. The tears touched silent wordless grief.

No one was in sight, thank heaven, as I stood there like a blubbering idiot at the turn of the path, altar wine still on my breath, the tones of yesterday's *O Esca Viatorum* still echoing in my heart.

PARTNERING

The great thing about collaborating at the keyboard is the sense of shared musical life, the exhilaration of moment-by-moment creating, hearing surprises emerge from beneath our twenty fingertips.

Picture it: the year is 1949, early spring in Connecticut, Waterbury Catholic High School on South Elm Street, a large, dark, three-story building that houses both a classical and a commercial side in its offerings to about six hundred young Catholic women.

In their navy blue jumpers and white cotton long-sleeved blouses, they arrive each morning at eight o'clock. Classes start at 8:10. Lunch lasts for twenty minutes in a small room with wooden picnic tables and benches where the girls chat over their brought-from-home sandwiches and milk bought from the ancient nun managing the cash box. The academic day at Catholic High moves non-stop, for at 1:20, dismissal time, after a pause out on the sidewalk to administer taboo lipstick, many of the girls from the commercial side head for their after-school jobs downtown. Some students from the classical side will head home or downtown; others will go to the art studio on the top floor, stay after school in some classroom for work or extra curriculars, and some will hurry down to the auditorium on the first floor for Choral Club practice or music lessons.

On this particular early spring afternoon, eight girls from the classical side file down the stairs, break out of line and dash into the auditorium, unload their homework books in a pile, and head for a piano. A music book is opened, the page found. Mother St. Reine, tall in her black and white, stands center stage telling them to hurry.

"*Vite! Vite!*" She looks anxious. There is no time to waste. The concert will be in a month and a half.

Two girls sit at each piano: the two uprights just below the stage and the two grand pianos up on stage.

"One, two, three, four," says Mother St. Reine in her definite, quiet way.

Eight hands drop to the keyboard.

Da Da Da Dum echoes through the empty auditorium.

They are off and running. Is Beethoven listening?

Mother St. Reine counts aloud, waves her black-sleeved arm conductor style, moves quickly from one piano to the next when there is a trouble spot. Sometimes her long outer sleeve dips over a pianist's shoulder as she points to a problem.

Now and then she claps her hands and stops them: "No. Listen!" And she taps out the rhythm. No one wants to be responsible for stopping; no one wants to let her partner down.

The eight students turn back to their transcriptions of Beethoven's Symphony No. 5 arranged for four hands, Mother St. Reine's idea for this year's spring concert, a tour de force. I am at one of the grand pianos on stage, loving it. Perhaps, I now think, it was a teacher's way to motivate less enthusiastic students. Who knows? This was my first venture into collaboration at the keyboard, and I discovered it was fun.

The beautiful variations of the second movement present a challenge. We need to cross arms for significant periods, the G clef person reaching her left arm over into the bass while her partner in the bass simultaneously reaches her right arm over (or under, as they decide) to play above middle C.

The practice grows wild, laughter explodes, partners mutter blame to one another, then get over it. The experience grows more and more exhilarating as days go by. Beethoven might have rolled in his grave, but I think not. Those long hours taught us lots about how the music works, and to this day, I feel I know Beethoven's Fifth Symphony better than any other piece of music. A transcription may enable you to better grasp how a piece is put together; scaffolding stands forth newly revealed.

Partnering at one keyboard is tricky business, as is any collaborative endeavor. Some temperaments are not, I think, suited for it. I love to collaborate and have been lucky with opportunities.

It is fun. You learn from each other, and you learn on the spot. That person at your elbow whose arm you sometimes cross to obey the notation, whose fingers at other moments tend to get interlaced with yours in particularly intricate passages . . . that person shares the resources of the keyboard you usually own. Four hands playing at the piano execute a subtle dance of respecting turf, listening, and learning how to breathe together, with each other, and with the music.

The basic rules of four-hand piano playing are straightforward: you each occupy only one half of the piano bench, separating just at middle C. The player on the upper, G clef, end is responsible to turn pages; the player on the bass side is responsible for the pedal. At times, accommodations have to be made on the page turning, but generally this is the norm.

How do you decide who plays which end of the keyboard?

With my first partner, Albert Spatz, a highly cultured man and a dedicated pianist, the decision was non-negotiable. For years, both in Germany and subsequently in New York, he had played "bottom," as he called it. He had worked through a wide range of four-hand piano literature and had a substantial library collected over years, some of it rare, a treasure ultimately given to a university. The albums of Weber, Mozart, Beethoven, Schubert, Brahms, and others to whom he introduced me bore signs of years of practice: fingerings written in over notes, erased, rethought, rewritten; emphatic arrows to repeat signs and dynamics signs. On the turning spot at the bottom of each finger-worn right hand page, he had attached a protruding piece of sturdy tape which stuck out from the page about half an inch to the page turner.

When I arrived on Saturday morning, he would have the pieces ready, the piano lamp on. We would talk a bit, then go to the piano and begin whatever we had agreed to work on the week before. Our understood custom was that we would play what we had practiced (I was often delinquent for I had small children at home and was trying to write fiction) and for the last hour or so, we would sight-read whatever we chose. For our prepared work we made our way through standard four-hand piano literature: Mozart, Beethoven, Dvořák, Brahms, Schubert, Weber, and others. Then, depending on our mood at the end of the first hour or so, Albert would turn to his music cabinet and pull forth original four-hand music by composers I had never heard of: Nicolai Von Wilm, Robert Fuchs, Moritz Moskowski, Serge Bortkiewitz, Max Bruch, and then perhaps a transcription or two, music from *Rosamunde* (courtesy of Schubert), a Bach suite (No. 4 in D Major) arranged for four hands by August Harn. Over the years, we sight-read our way through musical landscapes I've not heard mentioned since: a divertissement by Hummel, overtures by Von Suppé, a Schenker transcription of Handel's Organ Concerto in F Major, op. 4, no. 5, *Abendmusik* by Adolf Jensen and other rare delights. At one point, we decided to read our way through transcriptions of Haydn's symphonies. We did a few, but couldn't persevere. I learned about differences in transcriptions when Albert pointed out why he preferred those of Ulrich. The list of what Albert introduced me to is long and varied, but my most essential discovery was how satisfying four-hand piano playing could be.

What actually happens, then, when the two partners arrive and start to play?

It's subtle. As weeks pass, you get a sense of dynamics, tempo, rhythmic shifts in the piece, and you learn to feel those shifts in your partner; or, if you don't, you'll talk about the piece, the passage, and rework it, noting whatever you have decided about interpretation.

Albert was sensitive to touch. We would sometimes stop and discuss just how one of us wanted to strike a note, what effects were possible. Our tempos seldom matched the tempo indicated on the piece. It became important to move into and through the music together. That, of course, is the challenge of any kind of ensemble playing. Together you are generating a dynamic structure of sound, constantly in motion as it is being created. The notation is there to be read and its implications sensed, its possibilities realized, individually and together. As you play, you learn to breathe the music together.

For the past nineteen years or more, my Oregon partner, Gretchen, and I have had hours of fun at the piano and worked our way through some beautiful repertoire. We aim to meet once a week and play for about two hours. We're easy about who plays top or bottom and tend to split it, more or less evenly. Counting often saves us from disaster. This applies to any music-making, but when two are making it together, precision in counting becomes crucial. In tough spots we count out loud, emphatically, as we must right now as we work through Samuel Barber's engaging *Souvenirs*. Other times, when we feel more secure, we play along, sensing the beat together. And then, of course, there is always the ultimate arbiter: the metronome.

When we feel that a piece seems ready for us to go public, we invite friends to come and listen, promising to reward them with wine and sweets afterward. The deadline helps to focus our practicing. When we play alone together, we're on our own adventure, pleasing just ourselves. We come to know each other's trouble spots intimately.

When we play for others, questions shadow us: Will we get through those trouble spots? Will we have to stop? Will we lose count? So far it hasn't happened, although we have come perilously close. The nervous anticipation of public performance, even for friends, makes us practice doubly hard in the weeks before. Adrenalin helps.

As I write this, we've just moved into the after-performance season. Pressure is off, until we put it on ourselves again. For fun, we're been sight-reading through transcriptions of Beethoven symphonies, overtures to operas, reviewing old favorites — none dearer than the Schubert Fantasie in F Minor — making a mess sometimes, sometimes singing along, always coming away from it refreshed and ready for the next music-less hours of the day.

The great thing about collaborating at the keyboard is the sense of shared musical life, the exhilaration of moment-by-moment creating, hearing surprises emerge from beneath our twenty fingertips. We hear much that we don't hear when we practice alone. Now, in the doing, the instrument, the score, and our own years of practice coalesce into one transforming unity, all of it yielding us hours of delight and, we hope, some moments of musical beauty for others.

It's fun. It's exhilarating. It's challenging.

It is a trip out of ordinary time, playing as we go.

Above all, I feel this to be a privilege: finding a terrific partner to make music with, being able to share it with willing friends, musicking on a beautiful Steinway which, after a lifetime of playing on other people's pianos, is my very own. We play in a large living room, to our left a framed Gregorian sequence to the Holy Spirit — whose help we surely can use — and next to that a print of Chen Chi's painting of the old Metropolitan Opera House. At the far end of the room, large windows look out at a Portuguese laurel tree, and just past that there are the glistening waters of the creek rushing on to who knows where.

Into such a world of inspiration and beauty, Gretchen and I send our weekly musicking.

OF DISSONANCE AND TOUCH

There was a woman who longed, in some felt way, to transform her life into music. Could she explain? It would be difficult. The goal was impossible and she knew it. That made it worth the effort.

A MOVEMENT IN SONATA FORM

The first section in sonata form, called the exposition, sets up expectations in the listener by introducing themes.

The term "sonata form" can be confusing because this form may appear in other compositions as well, such as concerto, symphony, or even fugue. In any case, once the themes are sent vibrating into the musical atmosphere, they generate, in the ear of a Western classical-music listener, a sense of anticipation — we are going somewhere; the trip is about to start. And however many byways and sideroads we are led to, we will eventually be led back to a spot we can call home — a place of rest, the tonic. Final resolution.

For now, though, the music prompts these questions: Where are we? Where are we headed? Where can we go from here?

At heart, the question seems to be one of direction, but toward what?

The hospital room door was open a crack. We stood outside in the corridor. I could see, past my mother's shoulder, my father on the bed, a long tube still attached to his inert arm.

Distant. Unreachable. Dead.

My first encounter with the ultimate dissonance from which there is no resolution.

First and final theme.

My mother leaned her head against the door jamb and sobbed. Next to her I felt lumpy, awkward, scared. Her tears terrified me. We stood, each of us on our own island, apart from one another. Convention would say we hugged, but I don't remember. Clearer to me is the sense that her grief was untouchable, my terror a new isolation. Something inside me closed down. A flap on the heart shut tight.

She was forty-six. I was thirteen.

Four decades later, high on a barren hill in Dorchester, New Brunswick, Canada, in the small windowless classroom of a maximum security penitentiary, a pallid, earnest student in his mid-thirties peered at me through round, dark-rimmed glasses. We were discussing James Joyce's short story "The Dead." My three inmate students in English 101 sat carefully spaced from one another, no desks touching. They nurtured mutual antipathies outside of class, I had been warned. One student, Jean, an Acadian from northern New Brunswick, had recently emerged from "the hole," extended burial in solitary confinement. We kept our distance, all of us, touching each other only through words on the page, which threw a fragile bridge above the chasm separating us.

"We all think we're immortal," said Barry, "until we die."

Intense in class, rigidly moral in his attitudes, Barry would forever see life through bars. His crime was so heinous that even callous guards buttoned their lips and rolled their eyes at his name. Perched on the bridge of Joyce's story, Barry wished to explore a witty Irishman's exquisite verbal shadowings of death.

Avid to learn, Barry sent away to universities in Canada and the United States, took examinations in philosophy, languages, ancient classics. Some of his completed exams never found their way back out of that penitentiary. Mocked for his ambition, he persisted with the stubbornness of the desperate. Through works of literature, philosophy, history, he sought to let a crack of light into his cell.

On my last day of class, he waited until the other two had left the room. "This is for you," he said formally, presenting me with a new copy of Webster's very large Third International Dictionary. I had mentioned that I did not own it. Instantly anxious about how I'd get this heavy, oversized book past vigilant guards, electronic monitors, and metal detectors, I murmured a thank you. It wouldn't do to ask, "Where and how did you get this brand new dictionary?" Always a gentleman, he held my coat for me. As I slipped my arms through the sleeves, fear zapped me; this man could hurt me.

I carried the contraband out, no questions asked.

The next time I saw what had been my father, he was surrounded by satin, his stillness even scarier than when glimpsed through the doorway of the hospital room. I was up close now. The casket stood at the end of our living room, displacing my brother's drum set. To the right, a bank of flowers hid my Chickering.

As Father Cronin led the rosary before our final good-byes, did that dead eyelid flicker ever so slightly? Could it be?

I wanted it to be. No, I didn't want it to be. We would bury him. He should be dead.

I wanted life, not death. Song, not silence. Not this catastrophic dissonance in the harmony of our life. I wanted to be making music, my brother and me playing some jazz standard at one end of the living room. My father belonged at the other end of the room in his easy chair, reading the evening paper as I practiced.

I wanted to roll time back to the moment, four hot July nights before, when Mother and I, keeping our date to see a movie together, walked to the end of the block, then turned back. We knew he was sick; we shouldn't leave him alone. We came home to find him out of bed, watering the grass. It had to be done.

No rolling back.

As I went forward to my father's casket, I felt an unspoken pressure to kiss his cold forehead as a final good-bye. My mother had done it. I knelt for a moment on the prie-dieu. My whole thirteen-year-old being revolted. I would not kiss death.

He had beautiful hands, and I noticed them again, crossed at his waist, resting on his fine suit, a rosary threaded through them, hands that were, as usual, perfectly groomed, fingers shaped with a pleasing symmetry, very dead hands.

Forty-eight years later, in the time of my mother's radical diminishment at ninety-four, she suffered yet another fall, this time within the care facility pledged to safeguard her. My husband and I had come down to Connecticut from Canada to spend time with her. From our downtown hotel we heard the ambulance sirens. I said a quick silent prayer as the nuns had long ago taught us, for whoever's suffering the siren signaled. Then the phone call came. We hurried to St. Mary's Hospital, two blocks away. She had fallen forward and badly cut her face and mouth. Her lips would need stitching. At a loss before her conscious pain and fright, to say nothing of her stoic courage, I felt that flap on the heart close again. No words, no way to console. As she lay waiting for the doctor's needle, I held her hand and put my other hand on her forehead. When she finally could speak, she whispered, "That feels so good."

Later, when it came time for me to bury her, I would learn from the undertaker that she had arranged, all those decades ago, for my father to have a most expensive burial and had protected his coffined remains with a lead burial vault against the corrupting touch of earth. All business, the undertaker rustled his papers, surveyed again the record of my father's death and burial.

"No," I said. "No lead burial vault."

And then, "At the wake I would like a closed casket, please."

A barely concealed pucker in his forehead, a slight rustle of the papers again. I was flying in the face of established custom in Irish Catholic Waterbury.

"Some people benefit from seeing the dead body," he offered. "It makes the death real to them."

Why should the last view of those who loved her in life and cherished her vital spirit be the body of a dead woman?

The development section in the sonata form challenges a composer to lead listeners as far away from the original key as she desires by expanding the structure and exploring its harmonic possibilities.

Let us cross the bridge of modulation, then, to bind musicking, touch, distance, and dissonance as these have found themselves linked in my own limited time. Beneath these changes plays a *basso ostinato*, our resistance to finality, to death.

Run through as many keys as possible, stretch the sounds far away, bend them so that shape touches memory but raises a question. The challenge will be to find a way back to home key, but we're not there yet.

Oh, what a blast to find links, leap over harmonic fissures, then gradually work back to the second theme (in a different key now) and finally to home itself, the original key. In the doing, sounds turn upside down, inside out, harmonies are made smaller, larger. What a trip. Echoes abound. Diminishments occur. Time curves round and round and sends into life bits and pieces, motifs that emerge skewed, tipped, turned upside down and inside out from earlier echoing motifs. We inhabit an echo chamber. What is this cacophony? Where does it lead? Does it have a center? Does it need to?

The faces of death slide before me, so many kinds. And hidden behind them, cracking apart the darkness of death, the angel of music would tiptoe in to create, again and again, a sliver of light in my cell.

A couple of months after my father's death, I entered Waterbury Catholic High School, an all-girls school of about eight hundred students.

Now came the big switch to Mother St. Ambrose. French-speaking, brisk, portly, her small bright green eyes were darting pinpricks of alertness behind thick glasses. She bustled about, rubbing her large expressive hands together and murmuring "Vite! Vite!" as if life were too short to hold all the music to be made, so we had better get busy.

My tasks at the piano grew rapidly: learn my pieces, accompany smaller singing groups — occasionally, the Choral Club itself — and accompany singers on the weekly radio show. A new edge of excitement entered mere piano playing: others depended on me, others were listening.

I fulfilled my academic duty in classes upstairs, but I lived for the chance to run down to Mother St. Ambrose's kingdom on the ground floor. I don't remember ever seeing her upstairs where the classrooms were. Her domain was downstairs: the modest stage surrounded by several small practice rooms and the even smaller music studio that was her office. I coveted the small white bust of Beethoven that stood on her paper-strewn desk. By the standards of today's high school auditoriums, this setting was laughable. For me it became a minor heaven, distant from a home that felt empty and a mother consumed by grief. A musical heaven breathing with life.

The Choral Club practiced at least four hours a week, no nonsense tolerated. In the plain auditorium featuring only a simple stage fronted by four wide steps on which the singers stood, a flat wooden floor, and no sound system, Mother St. Ambrose packed in listeners from all over Waterbury every year for the three nights of the spring concert. Her Choral Club annually garnered prizes in state competitions.

A gifted student pianist, a junior, accompanied the Choral

Club, Claudette Chevrette. I loved to hear Claudette play. Her fluid fingers on the keyboard made the piano sing, and she carried with her a sweetness memorable to this day. I longed to become her successor, and eventually it became clear that Mother St. Ambrose was preparing me for that.

Claudette and I shared two deep personal attractions: making music and the religious life. Sometimes, on a late rainy afternoon, we would sit after school on two metal straight chairs down in the empty auditorium, our homework books piled on the floor, sharing our secret hopes and ambitions. Both of us dated, but that was a thing of surface life. Down deep, we dreamed together of living a life totally given to God. Was there any higher ideal to aspire to? Such a life would invest every moment with transcendent meaning; such a life would be open-ended in its possibilities for radical service and deep inner joy. We knew perfectly well that many nuns had weird foibles and attitudes. We dealt with that every day at school. But nuns, we realized even then, had no corner on strange behavior. Nuttiness appeared in all lives, our own included. At its core, the ideal animating the lives of the sisters seemed to us, in those long, intimate conversations, whole, noble, and compelling. We longed passionately to realize that ideal, our true harmonic center.

We helped Mother St. Ambrose prepare for the concerts in various ways: organizing music, practicing with sections, sharing the accompanying, distributing and collecting music. After she graduated, Claudette disappeared from my life, entering the Montreal novitiate of the Order that taught us, The Congregation of Notre Dame.

It was my turn to step into Claudette's huge musical shoes. There was no telling Mother St. Ambrose that you couldn't do something. You simply did it.

One wintry day in my junior year, I ran downstairs during my free period and discovered a sign on her studio door: "Until further notice, Mother St. Ambrose will not be here." A small curtain covered the door window. No explanation.

There seemed some dark secret about it. The auditorium, the practice rooms, her studio office — silent, dark, locked up tight. Upstairs, nothing was said about this. The next morning I sneaked downstairs before class to check. Someone had pulled the heavy maroon curtain across the front of the stage. I came in through the rear door and stood there on the enclosed dark stage behind the curtain. Soundless. Empty. Spooky. No sign of life.

About a week later, I was called out of French class one morning. "You are to go over to St. Mary's Hospital," Mother St. Mary of the Precious Blood said to me in the deserted hallway. "Put on your coat and go there right now. You may come late for your next class. What is it?"

"Algebra."

"I'll explain your absence," she said, and waved me toward the cloakroom.

The hospital was one block away. Light snow wet my cheeks as I hurried along, scared.

Nurses pointed me down the hallway to the room, its door slightly ajar. I pushed the heavy door inward, terrified at what I might face.

The room was darkened, blinds shut, and my eyes took a moment to adjust after the winter sun outside. I tiptoed in and stood by her bed, gathering myself against the shock of seeing a nun, for the first time, without her habit. The distinctive peaked headdress was off, and a simple white piece of cloth hid part of her still brown hair. Mother St. Ambrose's small eyes looked naked without their glasses. Her arms were out from under the white sheet, and they looked thin, bony beneath their long loose white sleeves. I stood there a few seconds, almost holding my breath. She turned her head toward me, but said nothing. Did she even see me? Then she reached out a hand. "I'm glad you came." Her voice cracked. It was barely above a whisper. Her hand touched mine. Cold. Then she turned her head away. Did she murmur "Pray for me"? I felt shy. The old heart flap was closing down. You never touched nuns. Physical distance was part of the mystique. Nothing to say, nothing to do.

A nurse slipped in and tapped me on the shoulder.

The next day Mother St. Ambrose died.

Eleven years later, now clothed myself in the black and white of the Ursuline Order, Mother St. Ambrose reappeared to me.

With a freshly minted M.A. in English, I began my first year of teaching as a nun at Ursuline Academy in Bethesda, Maryland. At last I could close a classroom door behind me and begin to discover, without constant supervision, what teaching was all about. I was assigned to teach English I and II and first-year Latin.

In the first week, the principal, Mother Agatha, a pale, sick-seeming woman whose occasional smile spelled effort, called me into her office.

"We have a sudden need I want you to fill, Sister. You are to take over the choral club immediately from Mrs. deSantis, who resigned yesterday with no notice." She tried to smile encouragement.

How does one get fidgety adolescent girls to stand still, forget boys, and produce music? And where do you go for material? How could I do this? I had no training. Still, one didn't ask how in those days. You just did it.

"Keep them standing for rehearsal, *mon petit chou*," I felt Mother St. Ambrose whisper as I gathered the girls together on my first day. Her pet name for me injected a shot of courage.

"Stand on steps of the stage," I ordered, as I set about arranging first and second sopranos, then altos.

"Make them stand up straight," the voice whispered. "Vite! Vite!"

"Shoulders back," I said firmly, obeying her heart whisper. "Remember, you are about to make music! Stand up tall. Don't squeeze your neighbor."

"Always begin with vocalizing," she murmured. "You know the drill, *mon petit*."

"Ahhh, ehhh, eeeee, iiiii, ooooo," I intoned. Could they guess

I didn't know what I was doing? That I was merely obeying? "Round your mouths, please. Put two fingers between your teeth. Like this. Don't sing from your heads. Bring it up from far below. Betsy, stand up straight. Mary, stop giggling. Is there something you want to say that we all should know?"

Back in 1948 we were Miss Walsh and Miss Kenney in school. By 1959 we had advanced to "Joan," and "Betsy," but nuns still carried the power of the habit and I intended to exploit this to the hilt. For an accompanist I found a gifted mother whom marriage and parenthood had waylaid from a promising performing career.

We worked hard toward the spring concert and the promised reward of a recording with their pictures on the slip jacket. As I see it today, that photograph tells only part of the story: forty young women in uniforms, white gloves, saddle shoes and white socks, standing erect and perfectly still in front of a nun, her loose black sleeves raised to direct them, her black back to the camera. The invisible part of the story made the music happen.

Yes, I believe in ghosts. Yes, I believe in resurrection.

The death of a life ideal is an old story. When it is yours, it is new. The conversion from one way of life to another carries its peculiar dissonances. What bridges will hold to carry you forward, and toward what?

The touch taboo starts early. Don't touch things. (I broke the China candy dish when we visited a friend's house). Don't touch that place. (It can lead to sin.) Don't touch that way. (The squinty-eyed seventh-grade boy pushed me from behind on a swing at the park, his fingers traveling up up up until my breasts began to tingle). "That way." Please, Sister, what is "up to a point?" What is "going too far?" Unasked, unanswered questions.

Fingers, hands: instruments of power. To be feared, avoided.

Yet they can make music. They can comfort. They can lead somewhere.

And when, during thirteen years in the convent, the rare

chance came, I explored touch on the keyboard and its power to soothe, relieve, heal, quiet the soul.

Midsummer evenings in our Waterbury neighborhood were humid, simmering with dogs barking, lawns being mowed or watered, neighbors chit-chatting from open front porches, kids playing catch in the street. Sometimes, after supper, my father and I would walk the neighborhood. A quiet man, he held my hand as we walked. Decades later my own son, who never knew that grandfather, would walk with me down the neighborhood streets of Sackville, New Brunswick, Canada, heading toward swim practice, or soccer camp, ice skating . . . anything. Hand in hand, we didn't talk. I let him seek out my hand, for I knew it would end. While it lasted, it was silent, tender.

These moments pass.

Our journey into the world of touching is complex, secretive, fearful, thrilling.

The learned Jesuit, revered preacher, eminent scholar, spiritual director, and confessor of many nuns, invited me into the privacy of his office at the university to offer counsel. "Would you feel better if you removed your veil?" His electrifying hands began to travel, past the crucifix in my cincture. Major dissonance. I left. No way to talk about this with others. Should your own shock torpedo the trust of another, especially another whose innermost life is grounded on that trust? Say nothing, especially when you know that other "young sisters" — as we were called at age twenty-seven, twenty-eight, thirty — visit him, too, and trust him?

Inside black, I was alive to the wonderful world, its varied ways to touch one.

In a classroom, other kinds of touching evolved from words on a page. Encased in their gray blazers, pleated plaid skirts, and white socks, our Catholic high school girls were caught in their own conflicts about touch. "Keep a distance from your students, Sister." But what superior or principal can legislate the terms of distance as you and your students explore Kafka, relish Thomas Mann's irony, Tolstoy's adulterous passions, Salinger's turbulent adolescents? How (and why?) limit the touch of literature on the expanding imagination? As I studied twentieth-century English literature in graduate school, my superior ordered, "No, Sister, you may not read James Joyce."

Back to music.

Years later, at Mount St. Ursula Academy in the Bronx, we took raw, restless youths off the streets of Manhattan to form a Diocesan Chorus that would sing, in May 1962 at Carnegie Hall. An ambitious project. At our organizational meeting, another ghost appeared. Thirteen years after she had vanished into the hidden world I now also inhabited, Claudette Chevrette returned. I had thought she was living and teaching in Canada. No. She had been assigned to a school in Westchester. For that year we worked together every Saturday morning with a mob of noisy, unruly teenagers and their ambitious, talented director, Bill Jacques. Claudette was still sweet, fluid as ever at the keyboard, both of us now living out the ideal that had sparked our deepest yearnings as we talked together in the empty auditorium thirteen years before. Partners in music, we still felt that deeper connection as we worked with restless adolescents who would make their parents proud one May day in Carnegie Hall. This weekly Saturday morning trip to Manhattan immersed us for three hours in noise, color, traffic, and the hard work of young singers hoping to transform their own cacophony into harmony.

Dissonance. A dear friend, unfortunately male, unfortunately secular, faithfully married, writes to me of his agonizing conscience problem: an affair. He is in love and deeply troubled. He does not know my mail is read. His slit letter is placed by my setting in the refectory after other eyes have seen it. His reaching out touches me. "Not your place," I am later told. "His letters will be confiscated." How can I let him know?

And what is that "place"? Jesus, I do not reply but wish I had, came close to the world, to others, who longed to touch him, if only the hem of his garment, and he touched them, spreading mud on blind eyes, accepting water from a Canaanite woman, letting Magdalen waste her precious perfume on him. He washed his disciples' feet. What is this touch taboo?

Darkness shadows the edge of all relationships. Dissonance.

"I want you to teach liturgical music, Sister, in addition to your English classes. You will go around to study hours and inform students that from now on this hour will be devoted to liturgical music in the auditorium."

"Go ahead, try to teach me hymns," their eyes dared me, furious at losing their study hour. After school, in those pre-iPod years, they listened to the Beatles, whom I had never heard.

Ignoring books open on laps, notes being passed, forbidden gum chewing, I handed out sheets with hymns transcribed into numbers. "Now Thank We All our God," "A Mighty Fortress Is Our God." I waved my long black sleeves, glared at whisperers. Their eyes glazed. It became a deadly, dreaded hour: one large piano, an untrained choir director, reluctant victims. No ghost appeared to help. The mighty fortress failed me.

Now and then, I'd put aside the sheets for the last ten minutes of class and dig deep into buried memory to resurrect some dated piece from the years in the living room with my brother at his drums, my father in his chair, my mother in the kitchen fixing supper. "Boogie Woogie," "Begin the Beguine," "Blue Room," "Sentimental Journey."

It wasn't the Beatles, but it was better than Bach.

The dissonance of physical pain invaded, slicing me at unexpected moments. We made our meditation in chapel at five-thirty A.M. Focus the mind and imagination on a New Testament scene with implications for your daily life. Sometimes eyelids closed and jaws went slack as we turned our minds toward God for the hour. Here and there a bit of drool was seen to escape and dribble down a chin. When the pain arrived, I would slip out of chapel, past the black forms so miraculously still sitting upright, even an eager beaver here or there still kneeling. When I finally reached my upstairs cell, the touch of my mattress offered relief. Lie here, now, until the time for Prime. Pray. A knock would come at the door. My dear friend, the infirmarian. That made her legit. Silently, she would come in, close the door, and sit by me, hold me round the shoulders, human warmth thinning the pain no doctor could diagnose or cure. No words between us. The warmth of silent understanding; an arm about me. "Keep your distance, Sisters."

All death is personal. It happens one at a time. We do not know when the light will finally go out.

For me it took seven years.

How can you sustain the sense that your life is turning into a lie? That a habit has become a costume? How face that in silence when others' lives about you seem reasonably content, reasonably good. But who knows what goes on inside the other life?

I went on intoning psalm tones.

On the occasional Friday afternoon, before we hurried to chapel at five o'clock for matins, a few of us, friends, secular teachers, students, would gather in the music building on the college campus. From the piano bench, I'd rustle up some music, sight-read, noodle around. Each of us had her problems: physical pain, the need to escape home, an alcoholic parent, a hopeless love affair, a sense of failure as a teacher, a bewildering loss of inner direction. We did not talk about these troubles.

I simply played.

In his *Late Beethoven*, Maynard Solomon recounts an

instance of music's power to offer wordless solace, to touch the heart with healing.

A dear friend of Beethoven had lost her child, age three. She heard nothing from Beethoven. That was strange, for she knew him to be tenderhearted beneath his gruffness. She could not understand. It pained her.

Then one day, uninvited, Beethoven entered her chambers, sat down at the pianoforte, and played and played.

After a long time, wordlessly, he rose and left.

A recent discovery of Beethoven's eighty-page piano transcription of his *Grosse Fuge* arranged for four hands suggests other aspects of music and touch. The *Fuge* was composed in the last year of his life. Filled with rub-outs, scuffs, blotches, the paper reveals the violent touch of Beethoven's hand inscribing the music, pushing it into the page, seeming to fight resistance. Of what? The air? The pen? The emptiness? The limits of his musical imagination? The fleeting presence and threatening perishability of musical inspiration? Of death?

His attack on the paper seems to pressure the paper to speak. Yet he was a master of improvising. He could trust the musical moment without notation. Still, how he dug at that paper.

Dissonance meets touch — through the arm, into the hand, onto the page, lifted from page by hand, into air, touched into an instrument, into vibrations, into sounds that sometimes would insist on their dissonance, on their not being what you expected would sound together: dis-sonare.

Even today Beethoven's *Grosse Fuge* defies analysis. It speaks in its own terms, harmonically, dissonantly, of life, of death. *Was muss sein, muss sein.*

Some deaths come slowly.

The breaking apart of what we feel was meant to go together, the loss of direction casts us into a sea of unanswerables: Where am I? Where am I headed? Where can I go from here?

One day Bach was in another room while his wife was at the clavier. Suddenly she stopped playing, leaving a dominant seventh chord hanging in air. Unable to stand it, Bach leapt up and ran into the room to resolve that sound.

So deeply hard-wired are we diatonically conditioned Westerners to resolve a question, reach a goal, seek an ending that will satisfy.

A luminous long moment brightened my final dissonant time in the Order.

It offered no answer to my raging questions, only wonderful release from them. This came from two sets of hands, friends' hands, at two keyboards. Sister Pascal was a gifted pianist. Like Claudette, her wrists seemed boneless, her fingers flowed over the keyboard. Next to hers, my own playing felt workmanlike, labored, earnest, chancy. We had been students together at the college. There, I had admired her playing.

Now we were professed sisters in the same convent at the college. I still remained mute about my dilemma. I taught, I cared for an elderly sick nun, I got through the days, and I prayed. Then, in the summer of 1966, when only I knew I would no longer be at that house that fall — though I did not yet know where I would be — Sister Pascal and I hatched our plan. Our superior's feast day was approaching. We would gear up to play *Rhapsody in Blue* for the celebration.

Still in black to the ankles, our heads veiled, faces framed by starch and white plastic, we rolled back our loose outer sleeves and set to work. The days were fiercely humid. I was a mess inside that cloth. When I could, after tasks were done, I let myself into a practice room and set about connecting notes, fingers, and my true friend, the keyboard.

Finally, on a steamy afternoon in late July, some sixty invisibly sweating nuns gathered in the auditorium at the College of New Rochelle to hear Gershwin.

I feel it now: the heat, my insecurity, inner turmoil. Would I find the right notes?

Curious to see if my memory of this great fun was exaggerated, I called Sister Pascal during the writing of these words. I had not spoken with her since I left the Order in 1967, but I traced her through a common friend.

"Do you remember?" I asked.

"Do I ever remember!" came back her familiar warm voice from a convent in the Bronx. "It was such fun. Terrific fun. We played just for the love of it, I remember that. We didn't over-worry about notes. We just loved doing it and did it because we wanted to. It was that simple."

She added, "I sensed you were having a difficult time. We didn't ever talk about it. You were very silent in those days. It went beyond words. We just played."

Less than a year later I would leave the Order on a dominant seventh chord, so to speak, and for a yet to be discovered modulation into a new key.

Echoes persist. Is there no way out of the echo chamber? Do the angelic choirs create a choral fantasy of echoes?

Years after the Gershwin afternoon, perhaps fifteen years, I was moving about the kitchen in our home in Canada. The children and my husband were out. I was probably scraping carrots or chopping celery for supper.

The telephone rang.

I picked up the receiver.

"Hello? Do I have the right person? Is it you? This is Claudette Chevrette. Do you remember me?"

Where was she?

"I'm living in western Canada. I can't stay on right now. I just wanted you to know that I've left religious life. I married. I'm happy. And I hope you are, too."

CADENZA

The cadenza comes near the end of a movement and gives the performer a chance to show off technical mastery. It delays final resolution, the return home. Cadenzas are improvisatory, echoic, varied, and unpredictable. What has gone before reappears here in new, beguiling patterns. Familiar motifs form odd links, surprising. The other instruments stop playing. All eyes are on the soloist. Everyone listens for instrumental feats of derring-do to blend harmonically with what remains in memory. What will emerge?

Where are we? Where will she go from here? Listen for the cue to return for the closing section.

DISSONANCE, DYING, TOUCH, WORDS, DEATH

She searched for the appropriate key, the way to modulate there. At every turn, the bridge was about to collapse. The words she had used so far wouldn't do it, the abysses were too deep. The whole concept of modulation, of pathway, of goal in the sense of key to return to, seemed tentative, questionable, oddly blocked, even dishonest. Of course words lie. And words about oneself, especially. How truly do we know ourselves, anyway? Isn't it easier, maybe even truer, to look out at the world we see and feel, take it in, search out words to make it felt for another, and simply give up those sentences that begin with the big I? The big I grows fat and boring. Music should never bore.

The block stopped her cold when she hit this variation on the theme of dissonance, of dying. It was set too deep inside of her ongoing, minute-to-minute living. It touched the question of her personal survival.

So be it, she thought, puzzling for several days. Months.

The movement in sonata form stood still. Words about dying and music simply stopped when she thought about him. Not to mention him would be to leave her story incomplete, unresolved.

She could not write about him in the first person, memoir-style. He had a right to his privacy. She, moreover, was still learning about death and life, still enlarging her ability to hear. How do you make an ending out of that?

But to be true to the music, she must say something about those long years of dying.

Finally it came to her, another way to sing it. She would tell a story.

There was a woman who longed, in some felt way, to transform her life into music. Could she explain? It would be difficult. The goal was impossible and she knew it. That made it worth the effort. What kind of music? Well, that would depend. Her life music would have pulse, a rhythm, a beat. It might not have a single overarching melody — at least not one she could hear — but somehow its bits, its smaller arcs of organized sound would offer her, and maybe some others, the satisfaction of music made and heard. Call it a musical memoir.

Well, then. The effortful bearing of life itself, having a child, sent forth one mighty arc of sound, not least of all the gasps of pain that went along with it and then, for years after that, the observing and loving of that other life becoming itself, generating its own music. Different from hers, she could hear it and recognize it as related.

Bringing life into the world a second time attracted her, but that proved impossible. So she would accept the anonymous gift of another, a life already sent into the world with none of her doing, and hope that her own inner music might find a welcome in the ears of that little being.

Years passed.

Many.

The tune of that second life gradually took its own shape and rhythm and pulse — in painful spurts. That other little being, as it developed, sent forth dissonance, dissonance, shattering dissonance. Occasional tiny bits of recognizable harmony caused shivers of grateful recognition in the mother. Even so, there seemed so little harmony he could make. No sounds meshed into decipherable patterns one could hear or read. It was enough to make a parent want to live with cotton in the ears. The challenge before her and her husband — his own music in another key, though related — was to support any music-making capacities they could discern in their strange new little being as he grew, despite his growing fitfully, unevenly, with gaps in his own growth pattern that not even the most highly trained musicologist could decipher.

Dissonances grew. Others heard them, too. Her ears struggled to stay attuned to what came from him to her, and as she absorbed the sounds, more and more she came to a place of extended darkness, a slow dying. She came to see how questionable the sanity of expecting, of believing in growth patterns, of trusting the normal. She felt the iron bindings around her hopes for motherhood: to nurture, care for, urge along a path she could recognize as the normal music-making of growing up. He couldn't handle the crayon, he couldn't bear correction, he couldn't sustain responsibility, he couldn't pay attention, he couldn't find a friend, he had no one else in the world.

He walked alone on his side of the street.

And then, after eighteen years of living together through the struggle for harmony called family, he found his way out of that circle of fifths and into the world of wider dissonances and possibilities. That he would find any kind of home key seemed unlikely, though she sustained belief that all things are possible.

Maybe.

And what was home key, anyway?

Time passed. She moved far away.

And then, the tonal link between them having held through all these years, their musicking arcs met again.

She flew thousands of miles for the meeting, the first in two years. She waited in the place that defies musical metaphor: the food court in a mall. Her heart flap was open and her own music quiet, waiting.

He had reached his third decade.

Then she sees him, in a baseball cap, worn jeans, an ink-stained khaki shirt, distant but recognizable. How expertly this non-driver navigates his electric scooter past and around tables where tired citizens take mid-morning break.

As he waves, rolls near, puts on the brakes for a slow stop, he grins widely.

Over coffee and doughnuts and as he expertly rolls his cigarettes, she sees that he is not unhappy. He sustains work. He can love. He can find friends. Above all, he can laugh. That is not new, but this laugh is deeper. He can look at his own life now. He has found a way to generate his own music, make his own harmony.

It is completely his, never to be hers. She had already known that. He doesn't struggle to modulate, he simply does it. He doesn't worry about music-making; he is simply inside it. Many years before, on a dance floor in a drab Nova Scotia hall, she had seen him radiate joyful abandon as he moved with his partner inside the music, inside the dance. He doesn't seek development, resolution, worry about a center or a goal. Still, she senses the pulse of his growth, the dependability of his rhythms, his repetitive patterns, their texture and color. She had lived with the dying expectation that she would ever find a way to touch his life.

And yet . . . maybe she has. When he laughs his eyes glow. He has friends; he is kind to them. He is learning how to love in his way. He is still alive.

And so is she.

The electric scooter has carried a gift to her. Now she can see, nearing the ending of her own development section and headed back toward the first theme, she sees that he has opened her ears to hear another kind of sound, life-making, call it music. Distance has helped her discover this. Intervals of space and time affect what we can hear.

Back then, thirty years ago, she had been ignorant. She still feels musically ignorant. She had not known how many scales there could be in the world, how many keys, how various the ways of tempering a keyboard to send forth tones. She had never heard of overtones. She had not yet been forced to new awareness by George Crumb's musical explorations, been bored by ambient music, been thrilled to Golijov's harmonies, tried herself to play Antônio Carlos Jobim's "Wave," or pushed herself to hear beyond the solacing structures of classical training to those structures that continue to offer her challenge and surprise.

Her scooter-riding son lives over there, in some other world of music.

At last she has found a way to write about it, include it in her memoir. Maybe his music-making came from outer space. They used to call him their little Venusian. He has stretched her ears. That can only be good. She writes these words with the advantage of time and space, years distant. She's given up the naive expectation of identifiable resolution in his patterns. It is not necessary. What on earth would it be?

It is sweet to imagine that we can pull the patterns of our life together in a way that resolves, satisfies, makes a coherent, pleasing ending. This is the composer's pride and delusion. Beneath such longing that ground bass persists.

What we glimpse through the half-opened hospital door terrifies. What we feel as we sway on the swinging bridge of words is a bottomless pit beneath. What we sense in time's relentless annihilations is the prevalence of discord, the insistent dissonance of death lining our harmonies.

Perhaps what we seek most desperately is comfort against life itself, its subtext of finality. We resist the heavy maroon curtain closing on life's stage. Yet darkness can yield to light, music's pathways can lead to places beyond present imagining. Touching a keyboard can reach the hollow spaces in the heart, and I rejoice to have known that experience. Alone or with others, at home or in foreign places, in chapel or in concert hall, with friends or with strangers, over many years, making music has led me to sing a song larger than me or my own life, pointing toward distant angelic harmonies wherever they may occur.

PRÉ-D'EN-HAUT

*In two hours on a late summer evening in the Chapel of the
Savages at Pré-d'en-Haut, two young voices sang of time's cruelties
and its renewals, a shining declaration on a hidden hill at the end
of a winding road in a small church at the end of nowhere.*

August 2003

Perched above the shining Petitcodiac River in New Brunswick
sits the small Acadian village of Saint Joseph. A single-lane
road leads away from pastel homes clustered beneath waving
Acadian flags and slopes up a long low hill alongside this inlet
from the mighty Bay of Fundy.

At the far end of the road stands a small white frame church,
La Chapelle des Sauvages, so named when the term "savages"
for Indians was not considered pejorative. Its red roof can be
seen as you approach, and next to it is a smaller white frame
house, empty, with a wraparound porch. Near the front of the
church stands a swing set and farther off, set back toward the
dense tree line, are rows of white tombstones.

The evergreen forest on one side, the river finding its way here
from the distant Bay of Fundy on the other — this remote spot

speaks silence. It honors the meeting of two cultures come together to build life in a hostile wilderness.

To the right of the church and down a steep slope, the waters of the Petitcodiac River shine. To this church we are headed on a warm clear evening. The concert begins at 7:30. It is one of several concerts presented here each summer. Now, an hour beforehand, the church is already packed.

Acadians chat and laugh, and the murmur of French envelops us as we make our way to a front pew and squeeze in. We are with Père Arthur, a beloved priest of these people, for a time pastor of the Sackville parish where I used to play the church organ. Now, after seven years away, we have returned to visit.

On many a brilliant fall afternoon in earlier years, I drove the boys and friends out here for picnics above the silvery waters, a time to be quiet while they enjoyed the swings or just ran around. I would stand on tiptoe and try to peek in the windows of the locked chapel. What was probably the priest's house also stood locked and empty.

This night is a special occasion.

Bruno and Aurélie Cormier, brother and sister, come from Chéticamp, Nova Scotia, an Acadian community on the northeast coast of Cape Breton Island. Their father, a lobster fisherman, is here with his wife of fifty years, celebrating their anniversary. Bruno and Aurélie left Chéticamp, went through Université de Moncton, then on to further musical training at the Royal Conservatory in Toronto. Bruno has already begun an operatic career; his sister will soon follow. Tonight they will sing for us. I, a stranger, an Anglophone, feel privileged to be here.

A buzz of chatter fills this intimate little church built centuries ago when many Acadians returned from their forced deportation in 1755. For survival they joined with their struggling Indian neighbors, working with them to raise this little beauty.

The Acadians have known the extreme violence of dispossession: property lost, homes razed, forced separation from loved ones. Theirs is a life renewal story that has taken decades to achieve. Even this generation, given, at last, the chance for education, holds in cherished tale and song the history of their ancestors who landed at Ste. Croix in 1604, struggled with uncooperative land, by Herculean labor diked miles of earth reclaimed from the powerful Bay of Fundy, and built farms and homesteads, only to see it all destroyed and ripped away from them by the English. In my experience, this is a people richly capable of joy, whose earthiness, to this day, warms me. Acadie. Its red, white, and blue flag with the gold star waves above most homes in this area.

And now, on a summer evening almost 250 years after their expulsion, their descendants gather to hear two gifted children of Acadie sing. Most of the songs are in French: "Parlez-moi d'amour," "Redites-moi des choses tendres," "Votre beau discours," "Mon coeur n'est pas las de l'entendre," "Pourvu que toujours," "Vous reépétiez ces mots supremes," and "Je vous aime." And then the bass-baritone fairly blasting through the windows, surely waking up the fish dreaming below, begins "To Dream the Impossible Dream."

In some sense, these vital, handsome, immensely gifted siblings are the living embodiment of what was once an impossible dream for their people. They are their song.

Clapping shakes the colored windows.

They are brought back again and again for encores. Her voice is gleaming silver, sailing high around us; his booms deep and full, a Wotan waiting in the wings.

Finally, to another hush in the packed church, with no sense of irony, they sing their people's borrowed story.

The adjective "heartfelt" would not be misplaced here.

"Evangeline," is a story of love, of loss, of unbridgeable distances. "This is their story," Père Arthur tells me in a whisper. Indeed, they've heard parents, grandparents, and great-grandparents sing, crying over deportation. The composer of this version, an elderly man from Saint Joseph, sits among us.

Here, on this summer evening, it doesn't matter just why Longfellow wrote "Evangeline." It doesn't matter that it's made up. It doesn't matter that the poet was American and from the Colonies to which over ten thousand Acadians were deported: among them Massachusetts, Connecticut, New York, further down the eastern seaboard to South Carolina, and further still to what would become Cajun Louisiana. It doesn't matter that it was composed in another language — English — the language of their violators. The Acadians have made the story their own. The song speaks the Acadian myth — deportation, exile, return — with heartbreak. At the end, silence stretches through the church.

Sudden applause breaks loose. On and on. Windows rattle.

In two hours on a late summer evening in the Chapel of the Savages at Pré-d'en-Haut, two young voices sang of time's cruelties and its renewals, a shining declaration on a hidden hill at the end of a winding road in a small church at the end of nowhere.

A beautiful nowhere.

Cantate Dominum canticum novum.

A GOLDEN ESCAPE

It was our weekly trill embellishing a monochrome winter, a musical magic carpet to fly us from wind and snow and village life onto the great gold-curtained stage of passion, love, betrayal, intrigue, murder, disguise, and happy endings.

New Brunswick winters can be brutally cold. Morning CBC radio would caution children against playing atop snow mounds lest they touch electric wires overhead. They were also advised to wear face masks against the chill factor lest minutes in the cold freeze their faces.

In such a world, few things comfort like the smell of burning logs crackling in the fireplace, tantalizing aromas from the kitchen, and the promise of rich carbohydrates later. Winter flab became our seasonal costume.

Snow could persist into May, so we sought to create a warming cocoon and eventually we found one: Saturday afternoon at the Met. Upstairs, Tom might be listening to his tapes, definitely not opera. Andrew might be outside sliding on packed snow or skating. We would close the doors to the living room, get a fire going, pull down

The New Milton Cross' Complete Stories of the Great Operas, read up on the plot, and listen. No supertexts to guide us. Just music. All that glorious "caterwauling," as one son still calls it.

At intermission, I'd set tea and something calorically decadent on the coffee table, listen, and sip. While stone cold earth outside wrapped itself in the snug silence of falling snow, we inhabited another world.

It was our weekly trill embellishing a monochrome winter, a musical magic carpet to fly us from wind and snow and village life onto the great gold-curtained stage of passion, love, betrayal, intrigue, murder, disguise, and happy endings. Here I was decades away from my first wondering exposure to opera in the Kenney household in Waterbury, Connecticut. At last I discovered why Mr. Kenney had listened with his eyes shut, why the rest of the family tiptoed around, why a finger was put to the lips when I walked into their house on Saturday afternoons — *Shhhh.*

Let the skies outside drop buckets of snow. Away from our home country, we had Germont singing of his home country. Healthy ourselves, we sipped tea as Violetta gasped her last. Distant from riots raging in American streets, we thrilled to Scarpia's malevolence and Rigoletto's despairing pain of discovery and loss.

This weekly trill played counterpoint to regular rhythms: teaching, writing, caring for sons, cooking, cleaning, wondering if nonexistent spring would ever come, and what kind of sweet treat should I create next?

COMPOSITION BLUES

In a flash, I was into a new phase of music making: composing blues. Compared to hours of drilling unfamiliar formations into stubborn fingers and brain to get a hold on rootless voicings, this didn't feel like real work. I decided to make a project out of this venture, compose a twelve-bar blues in each of the keys. This should keep me busy for a while and take me out of my comfort zone.

A word can function like a musical tone. It can unleash something unexpected, push you to gather elements dithering in your imagination into something more solid. It can even trigger you to act. A word . . . such power.

My music teacher, Julian, loaned me a CD he thought I might enjoy: Herbie Hancock's *Speak Like a Child*. I let it sit for a bit, then one day played it in the kitchen as I prepared dinner. In the liner notes, Hancock talks about "texture."

I like texture in material, in wall hangings, in sculpture, in salads, and especially in sweaters. Nubby. Silky. Gnarled. Stringy. Bumpy. Smooth. A mix. Texture can seduce. I like woven things of many bright colors. So the word "texture" applied to making music drew my attention.

Alongside other music-making ventures, I had just finished fourteen years of composing annual birthday songs for my granddaughter, Claire. During that effort, I'd not been thinking about texture so much as about words and melody: words to describe her growing up days, melody to sing those days. Now, though, I listened to Hancock, tamping down my appetite for melody. That evening in the kitchen I tried to listen only for texture. How do these sounds mesh, what's the tonal "feel" that emerges?

A few days later, drawn to the keyboard, I sought a new focus. The itch to compose was on me, a sporadic itch I easily ignore to read lead sheets, drill scales, or go through ii–V–I in the circle of fifths. Tedious. No, not that, I decided. Go for something new.

Try to compose something that involves only listening for the texture of a chord, a sequence of changing textures. How does it sound? Don't try to identify it, don't think in terms of tension, suspension, resolution, modulation; just go for the textured sound. Don't try to name the key you're in. As John Cage would say, listen "for the activity of sound."

Where to start? I had no story to tell, no audience to entertain, no melody bugging me.

Well, start with what you'd avoid like the plague, the key most difficult to read: F-sharp. Go for the jugular.

So there I sat at the keyboard that evening, one finger pressing down F-sharp above the middle octave, over and over. Fool around. See how many appealing tone clusters your left hand can make with F-sharp in them. Meanwhile, keep sounding that F-sharp in the right hand.

As you do this, listen.

Doesn't this sound elementary, mechanical, like beginning to read with alphabet picture books? I found it fascinating. Press down keys. Listen. Don't ask for more. Be still.

I went on like this for quite a while, textures changing with each shift of a finger. Odd fun. After some time, I found fourteen F-sharp textures. I stopped, jotted them down. Next morning, I moved on to putting them into some kind of shape.

Now began a new composing adventure. Little could I imagine then how far afield this impulse would lead me. No goal here to achieve a singable melody celebrating a child's life. At my lesson a few weeks before, Julian had treated me to a demonstration of the piano's enormous sound resources: brutal, delicate, mellow, tinkly, the spread of dazzling colors in between. It struck me then how wimpy I can be in touching the keys, how I under-exploit Cristofori's great invention. From now on, in jazz arrangements, in improvising over lead sheets, in wanderings over the keyboard, I'd tap into more of the piano's resources.

So then, texture, range — simple goals.

I began fiddling around with what I called Explorations in F-sharp. And I learned some things from this experiment in texture-driven composing and its value for me.

In the beginning, you see as through a mist, vague bits of something. Not a shape, just bits here or there. Something tiny, dark, extended, bright. Nothing coherent or sustained. Each shift of a finger brings forth something new: a few isolated dots, a line, a color. You work with the bits you see, or maybe I should say hear. Even though I do not "see" scenes or stories when I play the piano, this metaphor for my experience of exploring in F-sharp feels accurate. Think, for example, of Monet's *Rouen Cathedral* and *Morning Fog*. Little by little, the mist evaporates, a vague shape begins to appear, a tiny opening here, an arch there, recesses, some tall lines pointing upward, a vaulting roof. Colors — grays, blues, browns, orange, yellow, maroon — faint at first, then more distinct, emerge, fuse, separate, meld into his grand celebration of fluid seeing. The picture keeps changing. Harry Partch could do this in sound.

Well, I certainly was not composing a cathedral or anything large, but the analogy holds. What I could hear kept changing. Eventually, a shape came into view. And here the metaphor fails me, for you begin to see, or sense, or hear that your composition is lopsided, or repetitive, or tedious, and you start moving parts around, seeing if this next to that would sound better, create a more interesting tonal palette. Had anyone asked, "What are you making?" I would have had no answer. No thought of genre, of form, of subject. Just shifting around gathered sounds for the sake of texture.

This fluid sense of possibility and gradual emergence of form feels familiar to me from years of composing fictions. I am slow to see and reluctant to fix patterns of any kind too soon. It was fairly late in my writing life when the word "movable" came to me as release. I realized that when I could finally see the parts of an emerging story and had some sense of its driving impulse, I could shift those parts around. At that point, I would take scissors, cut the story into separate scenes and transition spots, lay that out on the dining room table, and play with it to see what happened. How primitive. How liberating. Surprises occur.

So, too, with my emerging sound texture. I've shifted, rearranged, moved chords and other bits. As I play it now, I think it's okay; nothing memorable, but satisfying enough. It hangs together in some way. I don't think it sings, but that was never the goal. It might hold a listener's interest briefly. It does take my fingers to the farthest tinkling reaches of the keyboard, then go on to excavate a subterranean rumble from piano depths. Rhythms mutate, a few chords jar, the ones I really like. They feel adventurous, new. This is for discovery, not applause.

Through these weeks ran the thread of Julian's initial caution: "Be patient. It takes a lot of patience to begin to hear what you may be doing."

One might ask now: what did you gain?

Courage, for one thing. Such venturing generates courage to launch out into the deep of musical possibility. It reinforces trust in the instrument's resources. And now, when I look at

Monet's several versions of that cathedral, see details gather, and the whole wondrous structure at last revealed, well, my analogy certainly limps badly. Dimness to visibility, silence to sound — that does hold. I learned about texture rather than melody, the value of sound activity over the vanity of naming.

I learned to listen better. I learned to hear more.

So much for texture. Thank you, Herbie.

Occasionally, chance tosses us a challenge that liberates unknown capacity. It's easy to duck that pitch or, as you stretch to catch it, lose your balance. My tale of such stretching and balancing in composing music loops and re-loops over decades. It starts in college.

When I left high school, my music lessons ended. Aside from playing popular songs for friends, my exposure to music at the College of New Rochelle was largely liturgical, leavened by the rare Saturday morning excursion into Manhattan to join the courteous Standing Room Only line for the Metropolitan Opera. Unexpectedly, junior year threw me a composing opportunity, a musical pitch whose trajectory over decades I could not then have imagined.

It was 1953. The junior class was expected to produce a full-length original show that would run for three nights in the spring. A trio of us did the major work: book, music, lyrics. Meetings rose to high hilarity as we stole from study time, dreamed up rhymes, doodled at the keyboard, and put together musical ditties we hoped were witty. All blended into the good-natured satirical book of *No Time For Laughter*, a spoof on the abundant absurdities of our 1950s Catholic women's college.

> We are oh so proud of all our rules and regulations
> Conditions, permissions, rule our days . . .
> Rise at three, take our vitamin B,

Exercise till sunrise,
Study all day, all work, no play,
Things are so worthwhile . . .
Our ev'ry move must be approved
By the very wise High Council
Which berates us, expurgates us,
As the case may be . . .

I discovered that I loved to collaborate. Our lyricist, Sue, had a quick wit. The writer of the book, Anne, had a strong sense of narrative line. I made up, notated, and played songs to go with the script. We rehearsed a lot. The evening of its first performance, our quartet of singing bridge players took off on their space adventure, were permited by the wary Wise High Council to land on an alien planet, violated its taboo against laughter, and rescued a young person into the world of humor. Lively songs, dancing maidens, adolescent lovers, bloviating legislators, cowed citizens — all that and much more brought appreciative laughter from our packed house. Our musical journey toward enlightened liberation was a hit.

Afterward, an elderly man with a thick, white moustache and black cane in hand approached me. "You must have been raised on Gilbert and Sullivan," he said. I drew a blank. Over sixteen years would pass before my husband introduced me to those masters of wit and song.

Someone arranged for the recording of *No Time For Laughter*. In its heavy dark blue cover, that collection of six vinyl records sat for years untouched in my mother's record cabinet in Connecticut.

In 1954, a few weeks after graduation, along with ten of my classmates, I entered the novitiate of the Order of St. Ursula in Beacon, New York. We had chosen to leave the world. This involved a radical divesting of all possessions. After two and a half years of preparation, we hoped to take temporary vows of poverty, chastity, and obedience. After that, if we met subsequent challenges, three years later, we would make permanent solemn vows as Ursulines. As we postulants began our training, we were bent on erasing ties to that earlier life. We would never return home, never personally possess material goods, leave the cloister only for health or education. We sought a new way of living, of being.

The fate of records from *No Time For Laughter* was far from my mind as I entered the Ursuline novitiate. I left behind the world of Sinatra and Judy Garland and undertook my own journey into the alien world of Gregorian chant, prayer, work, silence, and ultimately, religious vows. A new life began.

Forty years passed. No longer a nun, married now, mother of two boys, I was living with my family in a small town in New Brunswick, Canada, when that toss of musical chance again caught up with me.

In 1994 my long-widowed mother died. We flew down to Connecticut for the funeral. Afterward, cleaning out her desk drawers, I came upon a tattered envelope holding crumpled but still readable notated songs to *No Time For Laughter,* along with mimeographed sheets of lyrics, plus the original program featuring a drawing of the space ship that carried our quartet of singing college girls off to a laughter-less planet. Chance had sent me a musical postcard.

The songs still sang in my memory. I could hear those girlish voices laughing at their world. I could still sing most of the lyrics. Without hesitating, I carried this find back across the border to Canada and stashed the tattered envelope and the old records in what I must then have thought a safe place.

A couple of years later we sold our home, left eastern Canada, moved back across a border, across the continent, to Salem, Oregon, where I would begin teaching English at Willamette University. Once again, years passed, busy with full-time teaching and writing. Then, in 2004, now retired, I began music lessons again and shortly thereafter felt moved to write about music-making's gift to me across so many decades.

One day, poking through our largely undisturbed record cabinet, my fingers touched that dark blue hard-sided album of records. Curious, I went to the desk drawers containing sheet music. There it was: the tattered envelope my mother had saved. How unlikely. I went to the piano and played straight through them, feeling afresh that long ago fun of composing them. Yet here I was, all these years later, back to making and playing music in a new life, and even composing songs for a granddaughter. Back then, the idea that one day I would sit at a Steinway grand piano, in Salem, Oregon, at age eighty, again playing those songs, then get on with my current musical fooling around in F-sharp textures, was simply unimaginable.

We carry history in our bones and in our songs.

Once again, I did not discard.

After a little search, I found a local techie engineer who could turn the old vinyls into a CD and, with shameless satisfaction, wished on my son the gift of said CD for Christmas, and sent copies to my collaborators, Anne and Sue.

Musical immortality is not my driving urge. Who could possibly care about all this in the wider world? 9/11 had happened. The U.S. had moved into flexed muscle mode. We had our first African-American president. The recorded voices of young women at a Roman Catholic colllege in the Fifties carries no heft in a world of terrorists and tweets.

Then, last year, I mentioned this CD to my music teacher, Julian. To my surprise, he wanted to hear it, and in it found some charm. He encouraged me to post some of the tunes on YouTube. What on earth for? "You never know, " he replied. "You just never know whose ear these might catch. " Who was I to contradict that, I the F-sharp explorer, currently addicted to Albert Ammons, and mooning over the rich open spaces in Thelonious Monk's *Mysterioso*?

Grand total of hits by this date in 2014: seventy-four.

My virtual burden is light.

Just do it!

In 1963 chance pitched me another composing opportunity under the heading of religious obedience. After teaching high school in Bethesda, Maryland, I was sent to teach English at Mount St. Ursula, a well-established Catholic girls high school in the Bronx.

One early April day in my first year there, the principal, Mother St. Pierre, called me into her office.

She came straight to the point.

"Sister, we're planning a program for seniors to present to their families in late May. The girls will dance to the story of creation, accompanied by a reading of the biblical account. I would like you to compose the music for it."

Stunned, I stared at the full candy dish on her desk, reward for those who cast out their bubble gum and got through their day without chewing.

I must have squashed down surging demur. This was impossible. How could I do that? I'm sure I offered objections — inadequate experience, no formal training, limited talent, no extra minutes left from a full teaching load plus convent duties.

But we were trained to obey. God's will came to us, we were taught to believe, through avenues of official authority. She was my principal. That year, in addition to teaching second- and third-year English literature and first-year religion, I was teaching students liturgical music once a week, leading them in singing during their weekly mass, and teaching the nuns Gregorian chant for their Sunday Mass.

Surely, went the assumption, given all that musical experience, I could compose. How different was composing, really?

Just do it.

So with terror in my heart, I set about doing it. One did

as one was told to do. What comes to me now is a soundless picture: a finally professed nun, twenty-nine years old, even then beginning to question the life she had chosen eight years before, sits alone in the late afternoon at the electric organ in a vacant high school auditorium after the students have left. She can squeeze about half an hour out of the afternoon. To do this, she has skipped her required daily spiritual reading.

> In the beginning God created the heaven and the earth. And the earth was without form, and void; and darkness was upon the face of the deep. And the Spirit of God moved upon the face of the waters. And God said, Let there be light: and there was light. And God saw the light, that it was good: and God divided the light from the darkness. And God called the light Day, and the darkness he called Night. And the evening and the morning were the first day.

How can sounds evoke emptiness, make darkness light? And what music sends forth the spirit of God moving over the waters?

I sat there searching for musical tones. I remember pressing down the first chord and loving it.

Nothing more of the music do I recall. I do know that even then my efforts were grounded in those basic chords I'd learned decades before as I went over diatonic harmony with Professor Bonn. The rest of it was all from ear. I clearly recall feeling desperate. Maybe I instinctively listened for texture then.

A month or so later, the Garden of Eden appeared on the stage of Mount St. Ursula High School. The sun rose. Bright flowers glowed. Brilliantly costumed animals crept, crawled, rolled about, a lumpy lion roared, all erupted into joyous dance. Adam and Eve awoke, yawned, looked in wonder at each other and the world breathing around them. Somehow I found sounds to trace their tentative steps into that new world. Soon, every figure on stage was dancing, leaning, leaping, folding, frolicking in sheer joy at being alive. No Alvin Ailey here, but a good show.

Outside, in the other world, the Beatles sang, white-robed cardinals held forth at the Second Vatican Council, racial turmoil ravaged Birmingham, Alabama. Meanwhile, in 1963 on a high school stage in the Bronx, New York, creation began anew.

♩♩

My final composing episode began on Easter 2010.

Or did it actually begin somewhere in Europe in a cold monastery in the tenth or eleventh century? Or with bloody memories of Sarajevo, 1993–1998, and its long troubled aftermath? When we move to unpeel the onion of memory, we have to start somewhere.

In 2010 we were again hosting two young high school students from Bosnia / Herzegovina for four weeks. Promising leaders, chosen from their high schools, they were part of a group sponsored by the U. S. State Department to come to Willamette University and experience classes in democracy, life with an American host family and, above all, learn how to interact with peers they might never encounter in their country, families there still riven by age-old religious and ethnic hostilities. Memories of Sarajevo and its aftermath remained raw. Muslim, Orthodox, Croatian, Serbian — their high schools still streamed curricula and classes according to ethnic and religious background. Stories had been handed down about murders of parents and grandparents. By parents and grandparents.

We had been alerted that half-buried animosities might spill over while they were here, especially since the program purposefully put together with the host family students from different backgrounds. In spring 2010, two young women, a Muslim and a non-practicing Orthodox Christian, were our guests.

They arrived a few days before Easter. Although our two girls, Senka and Sasha, did not mark Easter, two boys in the group wanted to attend Mass on Easter Sunday. I agreed to take them. We walked together to the nearby parish church, St. Joseph's, while our girls stayed in bed. I looked forward to one particular part of the service, the still required singing of the beautiful sequence *Victimae Paschali Laudes*. I don't believe I'd consciously thought of this in years. Now, though, I could hear in my head and feel in my heart the beautiful Gregorian melody I'd sung and taught to so many nuns in my days as choirmistress. It was in me, as were other bits of Gregorian internalized over thirteen and more years, some from as far back as grammar school.

We settled into a pew and I picked up the hymnal to browse. There it was — destroyed. Wrenched from its beautiful curving line into 4/4 time and entombed in dull English, the beauty of the Latin blasted away. My visceral reaction caught me by surprise. I was deeply upset. The dismal rendition by an earnest children's choir distressed me further.

Afterward, we went home for scrambled eggs and pancakes, and I forgot all about it.

In late January 2010, three months before the Easter episode, I had been stalling time through a tough challenge at my music lesson: create an improv over "Stormy Weather." On the spur of the moment, I asked Julian if I could learn how to compose a blues. I have books about the blues in our home. I didn't want to read about it. I wanted to compose.

"Fine. Great idea." He turned to a fresh new page in my staff book.

"Here's the basic form for a standard twelve-bar blues." He quickly divided off four bars on each of three lines, wrote the basic chord above each bar, then handed me the pencil.

"Go ahead," he said. "Fill in something on the first line."

I stared at the chord symbols, the empty lines beneath.

"Just do it," he said.

Quickly, I wrote out a few tones in each bar of line one.

"Brilliant," exclaimed my usually understated but encouraging teacher.

I cannot recall another such moment in years of piano lessons.

"Go on," said he. "Just do it."

I filled in a few tones to go with each chord he had written down in that key.

In a flash, I was into a new phase of music making: composing blues. Compared to hours of drilling unfamiliar formations into stubborn fingers and brain to get a hold on rootless voicings, this didn't feel like real work. I decided to make a project out of this venture, compose a twelve-bar blues in each of the keys. This should keep me busy for a while and take me out of my comfort zone.

Scanning my few notes made at that time, I see some stages in this composing adventure. In the beginning, my little compositions were very open, i.e., had few notes in each bar. They grew more complex. Always a boogie fan, I was tempted to put a boogie in the left hand, so Julian made me a tape of "Boogie Blues" from the Twenties onward. As for my anxieties about composing the unplayable, I was told: "As a composer, don't worry about whether it can be played. Put down the sounds you want."

As I worked out a melody line for the right hand and then moved from simply sounding the basic chord in the left hand to trying other voicings and rhythms, I began watching my hands more and more, trying to get the left hand automatic so I could eventually improvise freely with the right. For the improv section, I drilled on scales to help my right hand improvise scalar fragments over a boogie in the left hand. Then I tried improvising over a walking bass, which defeated me. My notebook offers me this: "Drill, baby, drill!" Frequently, at a lesson I would hear a quiet: "Stay there. Try out intervals you're drawn to. Try all sorts of chords in every key." Over these weeks, I began to hear intervals differently. Eventually I had completed two blues in the key of C, then one each in F, E-flat, B-flat D-flat, A-flat and G.

I do not memorize music quickly. Years of sight-reading have perhaps retarded developing that skill. So as not to lose these rudimentary blues, I notated them quickly in my messy shorthand code. Once I'd completed the first six, however, I sat down to straighten out my sloppy notation. This took hours at the kitchen table getting it right. Which way do those stems go, and when? I was ruefully aware that composers today just press a computer button and up comes the form. This is not my story. Without such equipment, I needed to work closely on the page, Hal Leonard's notation instruction book by my elbow.

In the midst of this, one Saturday morning brought an unexpected phone call. "In about an hour a jazz combo will be playing one of your blues in an event on campus. Would you like to hear it?" Would I!

I hurried over to the auditorium, empty except for groups of young jazz aficionados and their teachers from around town who had gathered to show off their stuff. Up came my blues, the first one I'd composed. How weird it sounded. How interesting. Sitting there alone, I had the odd sensation of hearing sounds I'd composed take on new texture with piano, vibraphone, drums, bass, and a sax. Here was the activity of sounds, my own sounds made new.

I was living the shift from composer to listener, writer to reader.

As I composed my blues, I was still struggling with Hoagy

Carmichael. I grew impatient with myself. "Sing the improv," Julian suggested, as I stumbled and finally stopped. "Follow your song, like following a bird that's flying, soaring, dipping. Follow the singing bird." I tried it. Things improved slightly. Later on, in quiet times of my wandering over the piano, his suggestion would help. That day, though, I'd had my fill of "Stormy Weather." Outside of lessons, I was working on one more composition for my granddaughter's coming birthday, drilling ii–V–I patterns in all keys, and practicing a set of Mendelssohn variations with my piano partner.

Around this time, I mentioned to Julian my story about the Easter sequence. Months had passed since then, but my chagrin over the fate of the *Victimae Paschali Laudes* remained fresh. "That really means something to you. You should do something musically about it," came the astute nudge from an alert teacher.

Without a moment's delay, I burst out: "I know. I'll set about writing some blues based on Gregorian bits I've loved."

And so I did.

What a relief after "Stormy Weather."

I loved doing it. Composing the Gregorian blues took many weeks, but what unexpected fun it brought. That very evening, I went to the shelf that holds black books from religious life long ago and pulled down the one crucial to me now, *The Liber Usualis*, edited by the Benedictines of Solesmes, my bulwark through years of teaching myself about Gregorian chant. As I flipped through its thousand-plus tissue-thin pages, my eyes skimmed neumes, those little black squares on four lines, notation that represented decades of work by the monks of Solesmes. What I sought I found quickly: bits I loved, bits that still sang within me. The opening of the simple *Salve Regina*, for example, which we sang at the end of each day; there were two versions, the Simple and the Solemn, both dear to me, a soaring plea for aid in this valley of tears. The *Veni Sancte Spiritus* from

Pentecost, a petition to the Holy Spirit for light in darkness; the *Consolamini* from Christmas matins: "Be ye comforted, be ye comforted, my people" — heralding the approach of a Savior; and finally, the opening eight syllables of the *Asperges Me*, sung at beginning of a solemn Mass when the celebrant walks up and down the aisles sprinkling holy water on the congregation. As a child I would hope for some sprinkles to hit me.

Eventually, I gave each Gregorian blues an English name: The simple *Salve Regina* became "Help"; *Veni Sancte Spiritus* became "Come, Holy Ghost"; *Consolamini* became "Consolation"; the *Asperges Me* became "Sprinkles"; and my initial inspiration for all this, the *Victimae Paschali Laudes* became simply *Pace* ("Peace").

The verbal content of these bits mattered less to me than the curve of that sound, the remembered beauty of blended voices tracing song heavenward, songs of adoration, praise, joy, pain, longing: needs that line our existence. Though I claim here to have sought only the musical sound, how do we separate the song, the feeling it evokes, the memory it encompasses, and perhaps the deeper well of meaning beyond words that the melody sings in its tones. Think only of what, on a good day, can rise up from the singing of a patriotic anthem or a beloved hymn and you see how questionable is my claim of effective separation.

Stevens had a point: Music is feeling then, not sound.

To further attune my ear to modal sounds, Julian encouraged me to listen to Miles Davis of the late Fifties, his *Kind of Blue* and "Summertime," as well as a relevant bit of experimentalist jazz composer Sun Ra. I tried to move away from my Beethoven ear conditioning that craved tension and release, finding resolution. Composing Gregorian Blues covered many months, followed by weeks of notating. Resolution of tension was not the point here; composing the cry of human prayer was the point.

Translating the line of neumes from my *Liber* to the keyboard, I would sing the line, figure out the mode, then shift to the appropriate key, fill in the G clef with a melody, imagine something for the left hand, play the bits, feel them, eventually try to improvise in a repeat or at least over part of it. Urged to make myself improvise each time I practiced a blues, I fought discouragement and found that the challenge stimulated me.

Many weeks later, after I'd completed six Gregorian Blues, I decided to focus on three I might prepare to share with supportive friends in our living room. For my eleventh-century sequence, *Victimae Paschali Laudes*, I would first play the Gregorian melody unadorned, with just a drone in the left hand; then move into a left hand boogie, just once with the melody and then repeat the boogie while the right hand played a white note improv above it two or three times; and then finish with a simple return to the original basic chords in the right hand and the sequence melody deep down in the bass clef range, left hand. This turned out to be, I think, the strangest sounding of the three, and to me the most pleasing, probably because the melody of the sequence was unadorned to begin with. "Sprinkles" became more playful, with a tango in the left hand and the improv using the E-minor blues scale. Finally, inspired by the solemn *Salve Regina,* I worked with a left hand stride effect in my cry for "Help." A Fats Waller solemn *Salve Regina* — what a blast.

For all of these blues, I tried to make readable, accurate lead sheets. Aware of how strange this music is to today's ears, for that evening in our living room I would offer our friends the relief of musical comfort. For this I worked out arrangements of two operatic arias: the "Stride la Vampa," Azuchena's gypsy waltz from Verdi's *Il Trovatore*, and then, to further balance out things, "Di Provenza" from *La Traviata.* That bit of fatherly heartbreak would surely balance Gregorian chant boogies and a droning praise for the Paschal victim.

Our guests clapped. No chilly chapel here, no voices rising

toward ancient vaulting stones, no chanting nuns anxious over quivering quilizmas. Just shared pleasure over ancient tones reborn, freshly seasoned by Oregon grapes.

On hearing these Gregorian blues, no monastic nun would recognize the solemn *Salve Regina* in my "Help" as a twelve-bar blues. That doesn't seem to matter. Music thrives on theft. I think it correct, though, to call the source of this composing "inspiration." It is not really "derivation" or "copying" or writing a variation. There seems to be no harmonic similarity one could spot. Yet I aimed to honor the feeling that inspired each blues.

My story here begins with a single sound: F-sharp.

It begins with searching out texture in sound.

It begins with young women seeking adventure.

It begins with Adam and Eve awaking to creation.

It begins with exploration in an unknown key.

It follows a singing bird to improvisation.

It obeys a command: Just do it!

"Sing to the Lord a New Song."

No Song is new.

Every Song is new.

Catch the pitch of chance in life.

The future bears within it every past.

And now I shall go play the piano.

Notes

– Introduction –

1. Marcel Proust, *In Search of Lost Tme, Vol. VI: Time Regained,* trans. Andreas Mayor and Terence Kilmartin, revised by D. J. Enright. The Modern Library Paperback Edition. (New York, 2001), 229.

– Strange Relation –

2. Wallace Stevens, "Notes Toward a Supreme Fiction," in *The Collected Poems of Wallace Stevens* (New York: Alfred A. Knopf, 1965), 383.

3. Igor Stravinsky, *Poetics of Music: In the Form of Six Lessons,* trans. Arthur Knodel and Ingolf Dahl (Cambridge, Massachusetts: Harvard University Press, 1970), 51.

– Six Bagatelles for Dancers –

4. Federico García Lorca, "In Praise of Antonia Mercé, *La Argentina,*" in *In Search of Duende*, trans. Christopher Maurer (New York: New Directions Publishing, 1955), 63.

– Learning to Play –

5. Charles Rosen, author of *Piano Notes, The World of the Pianist* (New York: Free Press, 2002) remarks: (p. 19) "The danger of the piano, and its glory, is that the pianist can feel the music with his whole body without having to listen to it." Rosen offers trenchant remarks on the addictive quality of piano playing, its sheer physical pleasure. Thanks to a friend, I have recently come upon Charles Cooke's helpful *Playing the Piano for Pleasure* (New York: Simon and Shuster, 1960). His description of how to conquer

difficult passages by, as he calls it, "setting fractures" tallies closely with the process Professor Bonn taught me.

6. Josef Lhévinne, *Basic Principles in Pianoforte Playing* (New York: Dover Publications, 1972), 31.

– Composing for Claire –

7. Gerald Abraham, *Design in Music* (London: Oxford University Press, 1962), 5.

– Why Ornaments Here? –

8. Franz Liszt, author of *Life of Chopin* (Leipzig: Breitkoph & Härtel, 1859), is quoted by Jean-Jacques Eigeldinger in his *Chopin, Pianist and Teacher as Seen By His Pupils* (Cambridge: Cambridge University Press, 1986). Note 106 on page 123 explains that Chopin wanted these little ornaments to sound like improvising. Anita T. Sullivan, in *The Seventh Dragon — The Riddle of Equal Temperament* (Lake Oswego, Oregon: Metamorphous Press, 1985), suggests that eventually musicians used such "tiny drops of speckled dew" (Liszt's description) to obscure the sound of "wolf tones" before equal temperament became the dominant tuning system in western music (pp. 65-66).

– Improvising –

9. Richard Powers, *The Time of Our Singing* (New York: Farrar, Straus and Giroux, 2003), 186. See Rosen, *Piano Notes, The World of the Pianist,* (New York: Penguin Random House, 2002), chapter IV on "Conservatories and Contests," for a balanced discussion of the tension created by conservatory training that requires students to meet exacting standards and thus

de-emphasizes individuality at the keyboard. For remarks on the depth of challenge for a solo pianist as opposed to that for performing opera singers or chamber musicians, see Heinrich Neuhaus, *The Art of Piano Playing* (London: Kahn & Averill, 1973), 223–24. "Who shall help the solo pianist if he does not help himself?"

10. See Christopher G. Small, *Musicking: The Meanings of Performing and Listening* (Middletown, Connecticut: Wesleyan University Press, 1998), chapter 4, 64–86, and also his *Music of the Common Tongue: Survival and Celebration in Afro-American Music* (London: Calder Publications Ltd., 1987), chapter 2, for a discussion of shifts in understood roles of composer, performer, and audience from the eighteenth through the twentieth centuries. See also Rosen, *Piano Notes, The World of the Pianist.*

11. See Johan Huisinga, *Homo Ludens: A Study of the Play-Element in Culture* (Kettering, Ohio: Angelico Press, 2016), 44–45, for a discussion of the etymological and linguistic tangles connected with the words "earnest" and "serious"; "seriousness seeks to exclude play, whereas play can very well include seriousness." For a contemporary take, see Ben Ratliff, *Every Song Ever: Twenty Ways to Listen in an Age of Musical Plenty* (New York: Farrar, Straus and Giroux, 2016), chapter 13. Also see comments of Matt Treder on YouTube.

12. Small, *Musicking*, 9. The underlying concept animating many of these essays comes from Small, who sees music as an action — a doing, not a thing — and proposes an inclusive understanding of his term "musicking." "To music is to take part, in any capacity, in a musical performance, whether by performing, by listening, by rehearsing or practicing, by providing material for performance (what is called composing), or by dancing."

13. Nicholas Slonimsky, *New World Dictionary of Music*, ed. Richard Kassel, Schirmer Books (New York: Macmillan, Inc., 1998), 359. See also Karlheinz Stockhausen's "Intuitive Music" in *Stockhausen on Music*, compiled by Robin Maconie (London: Marion Boyars Publishers, 2000), 112–25, for a fascinating description of alternative ways of notating musical sound.

14. Charles Rosen, P*iano Notes*, 180–81, reminds us that only two of Beethoven's thirty-two piano sonatas were performed in public in his lifetime. They would have been played in intimate settings for a small group. Later, they became material for public performance. With the rise of the public concert in the late nineteenth century came a decline in material composed for *Hausmusik*, primarily four-hand piano compositions.

15. Christoph Wolff, *Johann Sebastian Bach — The Learned Musician* (NewYork: W. W. Norton & Co., Norton Paperback, 2001) 44. See also Walter Gieseking and Karl Leimer, *Piano Technique* (New York: Dover, 2013), 17.

16. Karlheinz Stockhausen, "Intuitive Music," in *Stockhausen on Music,* 112, *passim*.

17. To describe how Art Tatum exercised his hands, Whitney Ballliett quotes Rex Stewart's description from Duke Ellington's cornettist (*Jazz Masters of the 30's*, New York: Macmillan, 1972). "He constantly manipulated a filbert nut through his fingers, so quickly that if you tried to watch him, the vision blurred. He worked with one nut until it became sleek and shiny from handling. When it came time to replace it, he would go to the market and feel nut after nut — a whole bin full, until he found one just the right size and shape for his exercises."

18. Ben Ratliff, in *Every Song Ever* (New York: Picador, 2017), 149, sums up a fundamental attitude toward improvising that drives this essay: "Improvisation is a metaphor for doing what you can while you can. For not waiting, for making use of what you've got at a given time, which can be an awful lot or a crucial little." See also pp. 150-59.

19. Charles Rosen, *Piano Notes*, 97ff, cites the value of sight-reading music as a stimulus to exploring music. For practical advice on how to integrate sight-reading with one's regular piano practice, see Cooke, *Playing the Piano for Pleasure*, chapter 5, 141–44.

BIBLIOGRAPHY

Abraham, Gerald. *Design in Music*. London: Oxford University Press, 1949.

Carhart, Thad. *The Piano Shop on the Left Bank*. New York: Random House, 2001.

Cooke, Charles. *Playing the Piano for Pleasure*. New York: Simon and Schuster, 1960.

Eigeldinger, Jean-Jacques. *Chopin: Pianist and Teacher as Seen by His Pupils*. Translated by Naomi Shohet with Krysia Osostowica and Roy Howat. Edited by Roy Howat. Originally published in French as *Chopin vu par ses élevès*. Switzerland: Editions de la Baconnière, 1970; Cambridge: Cambridge University Press, 1986.

Geiseking, Walter, and Karl Leimer. *Piano Technique*. New York: Dover Publications, 1972.

Huizinga, Johan. *Homo Ludens — A Study of the Play-Element in Culture*. Boston: Beacon Press, 1950.

Lhevinne, Josef. *Basic Principles in Pianoforte Playing*. New York: Dover Publications, 1972.

Lockwood, Lewis. *Beethoven*. New York: W.W. Norton & Co., 2003.

Neuhaus, Heinrich. *The Art of Piano Playing*. Translated by K. A. Leibovitch. London: Barrie & Jenkins, 1973.

Powers, Richard. *The Time of Our Singing*. Farrar, Straus and Giroux, 2003.

Proust, Marcel. *In Search of Lost Time*. Translated by Andreas Mayor and Terence Kilmartin. Revised by D. J. Enright. New York: The Modern Library, 2003.

Ratliff, Ben. *Every Song Ever*. New York: Farrar, Straus and Giroux, 2016.

Rosen, Charles. *Piano Notes — The World of the Pianist*. New York: Free Press, 2002.

Schonberg, Harold C. *The Great Pianists—From Mozart to the Present*. Revised edition. New York: Simon and Schuster, 1987.

_____. *The Virtuosi*. Originally in hardback as *The Glorious Ones*. New York: Times Book, 1985; First Vintage Books Edition, 1988.

Slonimsky, Emery. *Lectionary of Music — An Entertaining Reference and Reader's Companion*. New York: Doubleday, 1989.

_____. *Webster's New World Dictionary of Music*. Edited by Richard Kassel. New York: Schirmer Books, 1998.

Small, Christopher. *Music of the Common Tongue*. Originally Great Britain: John Calder, 1987; U. S.: Riverrun Press; Middletown, Connecticut: Wesleyan University Press, 1998.

_____. *Musicking*. Middletown, Connecticut: Wesleyan University Press, 1998.

Solomon, Maynard. *Beethoven*. Second revised edition. New York: Simon and Schuster, 1998.

_____. *Late Beethoven — Music, Thought, Imagination*. Berkeley and Los Angeles: University of California Press, 2003.

Stevens, Wallace. *The Collected Poems of Wallace Stevens*. New York: Alfred A. Knopf, 1965.

Stockhausen, Karlheinz. *Stockhausen on Music*. Compiled by Robin Maconie. London and New York: Marion Boyars Publishers, 1989.

Stravinsky, Igor. *Poetics of Music in the Form of Six Lessons*. Translated by Arthur Knodel & Ingolf Dahl. New York: Vintage Books, 1947.

Sudnow, David. *Ways of the Hand — The Organization of Improvised Conduct*. Cambridge, Massachusetts: Harvard University Press, 1978.

Sullivan, Anita T. *The Seventh Dragon — The Riddle of Equal Temperment*. Oregon: Metamorphous Press, 1985.

The Liber Usualis. Edited by the Benedictines of Solesmes. Tournai (Belgium): Desclee Company, 1956.

Wolff, Christoph. *Johann Sebastian Bach — The Learned Musician*. New York: W. W. Norton & Company, 2001.

About the Author

photo: Josh Edelman

Ann Copeland has studied classical and improv piano during a long career as a teacher and fiction writer. Her books have won major awards in the United States and Canada, and she has taught in colleges from coast to coast; she was the first Hallie Ford Professor of English at Willamette University. Meanwhile, she has studied with a harpsichordist, an organist, and jazz performers; composed the score for a college musical; led a girls' choir; and shared a keyboard with a series of challenging partners. She now makes music with friends and family around her Steinway in Salem, Oregon.

SHANTI ARTS
nature . art . spirit

Please visit us on online

to browse our entire book catalog,

including additional poetry collections and fiction,

books on travel, nature, healing, art,

photography, and more.

www.shantiarts.com

CPSIA information can be obtained
at www.ICGtesting.com
Printed in the USA
FFHW02n1417011018
48643560-52613FF